Mind Expanding

Mind Expanding

Teaching for thinking and creativity in primary education

Rupert Wegerif

 Open University Press

Open University Press
McGraw-Hill Education
McGraw-Hill House
Shoppenhangers Road
Maidenhead
Berkshire
England
SL6 2QL

email: enquiries@openup.co.uk
world wide web: www.openup.co.uk

and
Two Penn Plaza, New York, NY 10121-2289, USA

First published 2010

A catalogue record of this book is available from the British Library

ISBN10: 0-33-523373-2 (pb) 0-33-523374-0 (hb)
ISBN13: 978-0-33-523373-1 (pb) 978-0-33-523374-8 (hb)

Library of Congress Cataloging-in-Publication Data
CIP data has been applied for

Typeset by Aptara Inc., India
Printed in the UK by Bell and Bain Ltd, Glasgow.

Written with the help of Julieta Perez Linares and Professor Steve Higgins of Durham University

Contents

List of figures

List of tables

Acknowledgements

There are a lot of people to thank for helping me with this book. I will start with Neil Mercer, Lyn Dawes, Karen Littleton, Carol Murphy, Ros Fisher and other colleagues with whom I have worked on research projects in primary classrooms over the last twenty years. In addition I must thank the schools, teachers and children that we worked with on these projects in Milton Keynes, London and Exeter and, of course, I am grateful to the funders of these projects for making this work possible; the Economic and Social Research Council, the Nuffield Foundation and the Esmée Fairbairn Foundation.

Julieta Perez Linares was a major contributor to the book, researching, summarizing and trying out the different practical approaches to teaching and learning that appear at the end of each chapter as well as reading drafts. Steve Higgins helped me plan the book and provided the first draft of the chapter on teaching strategies. A number of people have helped by reading and commenting on the book. Sharon Farnhill and Emma Smith came up with good ideas for improvements and making it speak to the interests and needs of practising teachers. Neil Mercer, Debbie Myhill, Daniela Manno and Anna Craft offered constructive criticism of aspects of the theory. Steve Williams helped me to shape the first chapter and to rewrite Chapter 6. Reuma de Groot made useful suggestions for additions to the ICT chapter.

Finally I want to thank the Graduate School of Education at the University of Exeter for providing a good environment for writing this book; a community where improving practice and developing ideas are equally valued.

1 Is it really possible to teach 'thinking'?

Chapter Overview

Teaching thinking is such an obviously good idea that you might wonder why we do not do much more of it, after all there is never enough good thinking to go around and we all suffer the consequences of this every day. One answer to this puzzle might be that we do not really know what good thinking is and where it comes from which makes it hard for us to design a way of teaching it. In fact some people have argued that it is not possible to teach thinking at all. In this introductory chapter I tackle the argument that it is not possible to teach thinking in order to outline what thinking is and also what it is not. Thinking is not a neat set of procedures that can be taught and learnt easily, it is much more like a way of relating to others and to the world. The child who is both open and questioning when introduced to a new person is likely to be both open and questioning when introduced to a new idea. This means that it certainly is possible to teach thinking but only by modelling a thoughtful way of being in the world: listening to children, for example, questioning them and reflecting on and even learning from what they say. Unfortunately teaching thinking turns out to be not at all easy because in order to teach thinking we first have to be thinkers.

Like all young children I used to ask big questions. Why is the sky blue? Why are we here? Why do I have to go to school? This could get annoying. My mother recently showed me an old primary school report in which the teacher wrote: 'Rupert is able but does not apply himself; when he is asked to do something he often replies "What's the point?"'. But this constant questioning was not just a way to annoy my teachers, I was very serious: what exactly was the point of all the things that I was asked to do in school? I did not know and nobody else seemed to know either. Unfortunately the answer I most remember my teachers giving me was: 'You have to do it because I tell you', which I did not find helpful.

Now that I am a grown-up and a teacher, I know how those former teachers of mine probably felt when faced with an inquisitive 5-year-old asking irritating 'why' questions all the time. Big questions from children can be annoying but they can also be an opportunity to introduce them to thinking. One problem can be the time it takes to respond when you are busy, but I think that a deeper problem may be that many grown-ups feel uncomfortable being brought face to face with their own ignorance. The first lesson for anyone who wants to teach thinking to others is to make friends with ignorance. It really does not matter that we do not know the answers, what is important is that we keep asking the big questions. That way not only can we stay young and creative for ever but also we can help children learn to think for themselves by constantly re-learning how to think things through again with them. For teaching thinking the right answer to every big question is: 'I don't know, let's investigate it together'.

To teach creative thinking you have to do creative thinking. This book is a support for anyone who wants to teach for thinking and creativity but it does not give you all the answers so that you know exactly what to do and do not have to think about it for yourself. For me this book is an enquiry into how education should be conducted: I hope that you will make this a shared enquiry.

Why I wanted to write this book

Going back to one of the big questions that I used to ask as a child: what is the point of school? My own experience was not especially good. I entered school aged 5 with lots of questions and I left aged 18 with some certificates and a feeling of futility. I had managed to pass tests and exams, but without real engagement in education. At school, learning was not something I did, it was something that was done to me. By the end of my formal schooling I had good grades on my final exams but I was left feeling ill-equipped to respond creatively to the real world challenges and responsibilities that faced me outside of school.

Unfortunately this experience of schooling is a common one. In his book *What is the Point of School?* Guy Claxton begins by documenting the evidence for the increasing unhappiness of young people in the UK. The figures are depressing but not really surprising. A 70 per cent increase in mental health problems among teenagers in the last 25 years, 900,000 reporting being so miserable they had contemplated suicide, 24,000 young people between 15 and 19 treated for harming themselves in the year 2005–6 alone. Guy goes on to make a link between these figures and the education system, quoting reports that many young people experience school as competitive and stressful, and a majority of young people claim that school did not equip them for the real world beyond school.[i] Clearly there are many complex causes for the increasing unhappiness and anxiety of young people; no one should claim that our way of schooling children is directly responsible. However, the mounting evidence that young people are in crisis should make us think again about our priorities in education. The big question that we face is: what are we teaching for and why?

After I had gained enough first-hand experience of life to recover from the passivity that I think that my schooling had left me with, I felt that I had something valuable to offer others and so I trained as a secondary teacher. Like most people who go into teaching I wanted to make a positive difference in young people's lives but I had not thought through very carefully how exactly I was going to do this.

My experience of trying to teach differently was not a total success but I learnt a lot from it. I learnt just how difficult it is, and I also learnt about the personal and institutional pressures innovative teachers often have to overcome. Since then, as an educational researcher, I have had the chance to work with many successful teachers and successful schools and I have learnt that it is possible to open children's minds and to expand their horizons. In collaboration with exceptional teachers I have been part of developing, teaching and evaluating approaches to teaching thinking that really do work, and that can be demonstrated to really work. Most of these approaches can not only be used to teach thinking 'in general', but can also be used to teach curriculum areas more effectively and to improve exam results thus keeping everybody happy, even my old head of department. As an editor and a columnist for the magazine *Teaching Thinking and Creativity* and as editor of the international journal *Thinking Skills and Creativity*, I have had privileged access to many success stories of new ways of teaching that have succeeded in developing thinking. I have also met and learnt from many practitioners who have succeeded in making a difference in children's lives. Now I want to put what I have learnt into a book that will be useful for teachers who, like me when I was a trainee teacher, want to make a positive difference in children's lives but do not know exactly how best to do this.

Why we need a better theory of education

No teacher wants to teach the kind of knowledge that will only be remembered long enough to be put down on an exam paper and then forgotten. Everybody involved in education wants children and young people to learn things that will be of real value to them throughout their lives in many contexts. Teachers who feel constrained by the system that they are in to teach for tests, but really want to teach beyond the test for skills and dispositions that are of real value, often turn to the teaching thinking and creativity movement. It is important to realize that the movement for teaching thinking and creativity is not driven by theory but by real practical concerns about how best to educate children. Parents, teachers and almost everyone involved in education want children and young people to learn how to think well and how to be creative in order that they can be happy and successful in life. However, a problem often arises when parents, teachers and other educational decision makers turn to look for guidance and find that there is no consensus as to what thinking is, or what creativity is, and little clarity as to how best to teach in a way that will develop good thinking and creativity. There is very little good theory around so those keen to promote thinking and creativity can latch onto bad theories that mislead and distort their good intentions. By 'bad theory' I do not just mean the slick commercial packages that sell copyrighted techniques as the answer to all educational problems; even academically respectable theories about thinking and creativity are also often quite unhelpful as a guide to good practice. Excellent creative thinking is much easier to recognize when you see it than it is to define or explain. The problem may be that thinking and creativity are profound issues about which we know very little 'in theory', whilst we already know a lot more about how to promote them 'in practice'.

If practice in teaching for thinking and creativity is often much more advanced than the theoretical understanding, then you might ask, why do we need theory? My response to this is that good theory is essential to promoting positive change in education for three reasons:

Firstly, theory gives us reasons supported by evidence as to why some activities work to develop thinking and creativity and others do not: this is essential to help teachers select the best approaches for their situation and to filter out some of the nonsense that is sold under the label 'teaching thinking';

Secondly, theory provides a story about what education is all about which can guide the selection of approaches, activities and materials and help justify these decisions to sceptical decision makers and stake-holders;

Thirdly, theory offers a way of communicating good practice to others so that it does not just remain in one classroom but can spread and be part of the transformation of education. (It is surprising how often creative people who develop excellent new practice do not really know how their own practice works or how to explain it to others: some good theory could help them.)

In this book, I develop what I call a 'dialogic' theory of education, which explains how to teach for thinking and creativity. Do argue with me about it. I do not think it is totally right, I just think it is the best understanding that we have of the evidence at the moment.

Every teaching and learning situation is unique. To be able to respond creatively to the educational challenges that face us as teachers, parents, colleagues or just as human beings, it is not enough to have readymade lesson plans or a few teaching tips, we need a deeper understanding of how people learn, and how they can learn to think for themselves. In each chapter of this book I will provide some activity plans and 'teaching ideas' at the end but before that I will offer arguments, ideas, examples and guiding principles.

A challenge to the idea of teaching thinking

Some educationalists claim that the whole idea of teaching thinking is misguided and that trying to teach thinking will all end in muddle and tears.[ii] I myself have been cornered at academic gatherings more than once by colleagues determined to demonstrate to me that the whole notion of teaching thinking is nonsense. The idea that it is possible to teach thinking, they say, stems from a naïve misunderstanding of what the word 'thinking' refers to. To illustrate what they mean they might continue that the way we use the word thinking is a bit similar to words for skills like, say, swimming, but while for swimming there are a set of muscles that can be trained up to help us swim faster the same is not true for thinking. The brain is not some sort of 'thinking muscle' that can be trained up, they emphasize, just to push home the point of how silly I was to have ever thought something as childish as that in the first place. Thinking is different from swimming or typing or any other skill because thinking is always thinking about something. It is knowing a lot about what it is that you are thinking about that makes you good at thinking about it, they argue, so there is no need to invoke a mysterious skill of 'thinking in general'. While swimming in the sea is sufficiently similar to swimming in a lake for the same muscles and techniques to be involved, thinking about chess problems is not at all similar to thinking what to have for supper. Those who are best at thinking about chess problems are likely to be those who know most about chess and have experience of a lot of different games,[iii] and those who are best at thinking about what to have for supper are likely to be those who know most about recipes for using what's left in the fridge or perhaps what fast-food take-away places there are in the area, if no one has done the shopping and there is nothing left in the fridge.

I know that the conclusion to this argument is wrong because I know from experience and from research findings that it is in fact possible to teach in a way that increases general thinking skills and creativity (I will say more about this below). However, the fact that the punch line to this argument is wrong does not make it a useless argument. It is true that thinking is always thinking about something and that it is hard to separate out the thinking from the something that is being thought about in order to teach the one without at the same time teaching the other. Good arguments for wrong conclusions are useful for teaching thinking because they make us question our assumptions. If on our normal view of thinking it should not be possible to teach thinking then that might mean that we should re-think what we mean by thinking. In the next few sections of this chapter I will look at some popular metaphors for thinking in order to question them and develop a better theory of what thinking is and of how we can teach for thinking.

Metaphors for thinking and teaching thinking

Theories are stories about how things fit together that use things that we already understand in order to explain things that we do not yet understand. This is why theories are all based originally on metaphors drawn from experience. This is true in every area of science: in biology the breakthrough theory of the circulation of the blood depended on applying the metaphor of the heart as a pump, in physics Rutherford understood the structure of atoms on the model of the solar system with electrons circulating around a central nucleus like planets circulating around the sun, in chemistry the benzene molecule ring structure was only discovered by Kekulé after he had a dream about a snake eating its own tail. The metaphor we adopt determines what questions we ask and what seems like a convincing answer and so it is important to dig up and think about the metaphors of thinking that lie behind approaches to teaching thinking.

I want to propose a dialogic theory of thinking and teaching thinking, which starts from the metaphor of thinking as dialogue. To explain why this is of more use than all the other theories that are around I will look briefly at their underlying metaphors in order to show why these metaphors are of limited relevance. The three key metaphors most popular at the moment are: thinking as the activity of a machine, thinking as the activity of the brain and thinking as the use of cultural tools.

1 The metaphor of the thinking machine

From the moment people started building complex machines they started speculating that perhaps our own thinking works in a similar way. In the seventeenth century the first really accurate pocket watches were constructed for use in navigating long ocean voyages and around the same time the image of clockwork came to be used routinely as a metaphor for the workings of the mind. This association of clockwork with thinking was greatly helped by the construction of clockwork calculating machines first by Blaise Pascal (1642), then by Leibniz (1673) and later, and most magnificently, by Charles Babbage in London (1822). Babbage's analytic engine contained thousands of shiny brass cog wheels and could perform all sorts of mathematical calculations. He saw it as a model of how the mind worked and this image of the mind as complexly related cog wheels entered the popular imagination.

The psychologist who has perhaps had most influence on ideas of the development of thinking in education is Jean Piaget. His ideas are complicated and it might seem rather dismissive and superficial to suggest that they are all based on the metaphor of the mind as clockwork (especially since he came from Switzerland which is famous for watch making and his family name is also given to a famous brand of Swiss watches). On the other hand his theory of how intelligence grows depends on positing underlying 'cognitive structures' and inner mechanisms like 'equilibration' which determine how these cognitive structures develop. What exactly does Piaget have in mind when he writes of 'cognitive structures', 'equilibration' and other similar terms? I find it hard to visualize these without thinking of machinery like cogs and springs all working perfectly together.

On Piaget's theory intelligent thinking evolves and adapts to the environment. Children interact with their environment and discover new facts. An 'equilibration' system determines whether each new fact can fit with existing cognitive structures (assimilation) or whether those structures need to change to fit the new facts (accommodation). He proposes a stage theory of development as the underlying cognitive structures of thinking unfold to be more and more logical and universal. Piaget admits that sometimes children who have reached the more logical stage of thinking ('formal-operational') respond in ways that do not fit that stage and he refers to this effect as 'horizontal decollage' or slippage.

Robert Sternberg, a well known authority in the field of the psychology of intelligence, is very sympathetic to Piaget, but he points out that the experimental evidence gathered in the eighty years or so since Piaget first put forward this theory has given it a 'battering'.[iv] Like Babbage's clockwork machine Piaget's model can only address formal logical thinking and most experts now agree that intelligence requires creativity and imagination more than formal analysis. Research also does not support his claims about the stages of intellectual development. In reality how children think, just like how adults think, depends more on the context of their thinking than on their supposed stage of cognitive development. This is not a surprise if we look at our experience of thinking. We must all know people who can think logically in one context, say talking to their bank manager about a loan, but fail to think logically in another context, say when dealing with emotional issues in close relationships.

Piaget's developmental constructivism is a very different tradition of thinking about thinking from the computer model of mind that came to dominate cognitive psychology in the 1960s. However, I think that they are similar in that both share an underlying metaphor of the mind as a thinking machine. On the computer metaphor the brain is seen as like the hardware of a computer and thinking is seen as a software process. Many psychologists think that this model has proved hugely productive in understanding the way that the mind works. It has proved useful for understanding effects like the 'working memory' whereby we can only consciously handle a limited number of bits of information at a time. However, it has failed to address the central problem of teaching thinking: how do we understand and promote high quality thinking? Computer based models of problem solving and creativity work only when we know in advance what would count as a solution to the problem and what the rules are for thinking about it. Chess is a good example of the sort of thinking computers can address because in chess we know what it means to win the game (to checkmate the opponent) and we know exactly what moves are allowed and what moves are not allowed. Computer programs have proved good at playing chess in ways that mimic some of the strategies of good human players. That is a major achievement. In the real world, however, we mostly have to think even when we do not know what will be the solution when we start out and we often have to change the rules as we go along. Many dialogues are complex and open-ended in a way that cannot be simulated by a computer program. For example, when a research team sits down together to discuss progress on a project they may not know in advance what the problems are let alone what the solutions will turn out to be; the problems and the solutions often emerge in the course of the meeting. The main 'rule' of successful problem solving often turns out to be seeing the problem in a completely new and unexpected way that helps reveal its solution (see Chapter 4). This is not the sort of rule that a computer program can simulate.

2 The metaphor of thinking as the activity of the brain

Some argue that rather than trying to understand thinking through computer models we should look directly at real thinking as it happens in the brain. This approach is made possible by new brain scanning techniques such as Magnetic Resonance Imaging (MRI) and Positron Emission Tomography (PET). These measures can show brain activity when subjects are doing different tasks. Some of the findings of brain science are quite useful for education. It is useful to know, for instance, that the brain appears to learn things even when we are not paying attention to them.[v] Other findings are highly evocative like the discovery of mirror neurons that generate the same feelings in us when we observe others acting in a certain way that we would feel if we were acting in that way. This sort of work shows promise but the experts all agree that it is still very limited in what it can show for normal human creative thinking.

This modesty from the experts is interesting because there is already a small industry of teaching thinking approaches that claim to be based upon brain research but are in fact quite spurious. In one brain-based education book I read that greeting children at the door of the class 'soothes the reptile brain', as if anyone really knows that. Can we not just intuit from experience that greeting children by name at the door of the class is good practice regardless of the reptile brain?[vi]

Many people assume that it is simply a fact that thinking occurs in the brain and when we look at brain activity we are looking directly at thinking. It might therefore seem odd that I am treating 'the activity of the brain' as another metaphor of thinking. I think that brain activity is a metaphor for thinking rather than the real thing partly because there is a philosophical problem with the view that when we look at brain activity we are looking directly at thinking. This problem is often expressed in the form of a paradox: the world is in the brain but the brain is in the world. Max Velmans, a psychologist specializing in consciousness, suggests we try the experiment of sticking a pin hard in our little finger to illustrate this paradox. If we do this it is clear that the pain occurs in the little finger. It adds nothing useful to say that the pain occurs somewhere 'in the brain'. If we were able to observe the brain at the same time that we stick the pin in the finger there might be some correlated activity but it is not the same thing as the real pain that we feel in our finger. In a similar way thinking may well be correlated with observed brain activity but that observed activity is not the same thing as the thinking. Velmans' solution to the puzzle that the world is in the brain while the brain is in the world is to claim that there must be a prior generation of a 'world for us' out of an interaction between the organism and its environment. The word 'prior' here is used logically in the sense that before we experience a world in space and time with things like fingers and brains in it, there must be some sort of construction process going on behind the scenes.[vii] The best analogy I can think of for this is the old fashioned vinyl gramophone record and the needle that produces music when the record is turned. As the needle moves up and down along the grooves in the record, music is generated and forms its own world of feelings and patterns of sound. In a similar way a 'prior interaction' between us and the real world generates the world we see and experience. Thinking seems to be part of that 'prior interaction'. Thinking is not therefore simply some sort of external physical activity that we can observe in the world just as we can observe neuronal activity in the brain. Thinking also helps us to construct a 'world for us' in the first place and part of that 'world for us' includes our images of the brain and of brain activity and theories about neurons and so on.

Thinking that we are reducible to observable brain activity is a bit like the mistake we might make when we look at ourselves in a mirror and we think that the image is us. Actually it is not us because we are the ones looking at the image and the image is not really looking at us, it just seems to be. The living act of looking out at the world and responding to what we see is far more important to who we are than the image of our physical body that we see in the mirror staring back at us. In a similar way the living act of thinking, when we are thinking about thinking, is the real thing, and the image or idea or theory of thinking that we construct in our 'mind's eye' or write down on paper is always an external trace or echo or shadow of this real thinking.

To help teach thinking we need a theory that understands thinking from the inside, 'in the act' as it were. This does not mean that looking at thinking from the outside is useless. Brain research shows, for example, that a child whose brain lacks sufficient water will often do less well at critical and creative thinking tasks than they would otherwise. In this case it is clear that understanding the external physical conditions of high quality thinking can help us promote more high quality thinking, if only by making sure children have water easily available in schools. Brain research helps in this way by revealing the conditions of thinking but it cannot offer a theory of thinking itself because thinking is not an external thing in an already existing world but an internal action that generates the 'world for us' in the first place.

This distinction between external knowledge of thinking as a brain process and the internal reality of thinking is important so I will give a concrete example to help convince you of the argument. Imagine a 10-year-old girl having her brain scanned while the poem '*Tyger! Tyger! burning bright*' is read to her. This poem by William Blake is a favourite with children but it is also potentially a profound spur to thinking. In it Blake asks what kind of creator God would make something as fierce and cruel as the tiger and asks: '*Did he smile his work to see? Did he who made the Lamb make thee?*'. To feel the intellectual force of this challenge to complacent ways of talking about 'the harmony of nature' is already to be deeply engaged in the action of thinking. A theory of thinking that could help us teach thinking needs to be able to offer guidance as to how teachers could draw children into Blake's vision of reality so that they can both understand his vision for themselves and yet be able to question it. Knowing in detail which neurons fired in the child's brain at each word in the reading will never help us understand this kind of thinking nor how to promote it. Like Blake's poem, thinking is something that we need to understand and work with from the inside.

3 The metaphor of thinking as the use of cultural tools

The computer metaphor of mind implies that good thinking everywhere is pretty much the same in following certain abstract logical laws or general problem-solving patterns. The evidence does not support this view. Socio-cultural theory claims, by contrast, that thinking always occurs in a situation where it is 'mediated' by cultural tools and practices. For example, the way in which young children solve maths problems like division, and the mistakes that they make solving the problems reveal the cultural tools that they are using. Sometimes they get out a pen and some paper and show their working out with diagrams, columns and rows and sometimes they work out the problems in their heads silently, but either way they can be said to be using cultural tools.[viii]

This socio-cultural approach is often associated with a rejection of the idea of teaching thinking in general precisely because the concept of thinking in general no longer makes sense if we use this metaphor. All we have, according to this metaphor, are specific sets of cultural tools to help with specific cultural activities. No one learns 'thinking in general', they claim, but one person might learn how to use the symbols and tools of mathematics to think as a mathematician while another person might learn how to think as a fisherman using tools to navigate and cultural knowledge to find good fishing grounds. However, the aspiration to teach thinking in general can perhaps be rescued in the form of teaching learners how to use cultural tools that can be applied across a range of contexts. Particular 'educated' ways of talking together, including 'Exploratory Talk', defined through social ground rules such as questioning claims, giving reasons, seeking agreement and so on, have been offered as a 'cultural tool' that is effective in supporting thinking in many contexts.[ix] In the 'Exploratory Talk' approach to teaching thinking the 'cultural tool' can be said to be a way of using words that can be taught and learnt.

4 The metaphor of thinking as dialogue

All the metaphors of thinking that we have looked at so far – thinking as like a computer, thinking as the activity of the brain, thinking as tool use – have something useful to say about thinking but all are limited because they assume an external view of thinking. Thinking is an internal reality first so whatever we observe externally, be it a computer model, a pattern of colour in a PET brain scan or the transcript of a dialogue, are traces of thinking after the event. Thinking itself must always be somehow 'bigger' than these traces because they are all thoughts about thinking and not the reality of thinking itself. We are always already thinking on the inside, thinking in the act, and this intimacy we have with thinking on the inside should give us some intuitions into its nature.

Those who have tried hardest to observe themselves in the act of thinking and describe its nature conclude that it is like a dialogue. Heidegger for instance wrote a book on thinking in which he claims that we think not because we have problems to solve so much as because something or someone calls us to think; he writes that we are called to think by that which is most thought provoking for us.[x] A philosopher being called to think by that which is most thought provoking is not in a dialogue exactly, in the normal sense of the word, because there is no one else physically present. However, since this kind of thinking takes the form of a dialogue we can call this understanding of thinking 'dialogic'. Real spoken dialogues can be thoughtful, like those Socrates had with his friends and students, but internal silent thoughts often also take the form of dialogues. For example, when I read Plato describing the dialogues that Socrates had, this stimulates me to respond with thoughts of my own that feel to me to be like a dialogue with Socrates. When I try to observe my own thinking it feels more like an internal dialogue between different voices than it feels like a mechanical operation of 'cognitive structures' or computer programs, or like an operation of my brain or indeed like the use of cultural tools.

When I am called out by you in a dialogue to see from your perspective I do not lose myself completely but I can see things from two perspectives at once, my own and yours. However, I can never actually be you and see things exactly as you see them which means that there is a tension in every dialogue which is the tension of holding two or more positions that cannot simply be combined into one. Out of that tension between perspectives or points of view comes criticism and judgement but also insight and understanding. It is this tension that drives thinking, which is why all human thinking is at source creative thinking. Michael Bakhtin, one of the originators of this dialogic perspective, described how his reading of ancient Greek texts helped him to understand his situation in Russia in the early twentieth century in a new light. Each thought is seeing something 'as if' from the point of view of another person and longer stretches of thinking are like a play of voices or perspectives. For dialogic theory, learning to think means being pulled out of oneself to take the perspectives of other people and, through that engagement in a play of perspectives, to be able to creatively generate new perspectives or ways of seeing and thinking about the world.

So what is thinking?

When people write and talk about 'teaching thinking' they do not just mean teaching any old thinking because some thinking is obviously quite bad. They mean teaching 'good thinking' which roughly translates as 'the kind of thinking that we want to see more of'. One problem with defining good thinking is that each metaphor of thinking tends to imply its own definition of good thinking. For instance, the clockwork and computer metaphors of mind imply that good thinking is formal logical thinking. However, formal logical thinking may not be the sort of thinking that is seen as of most use to people in many real world situations. There is no way to be completely 'objective' about good thinking but one way to try is to ask lots of people what they think. Lauren Resnick chaired a government enquiry into teaching thinking in the USA and asked many expert teachers what they understood by excellent thinking or 'Higher Order Thinking' of the kind that they wanted to teach. She concluded that Higher Order Thinking was hard to define in advance because it was surprising. In her final report she wrote:

> Thinking skills resist the precise forms of definition we have come to associate with the setting of specified objectives for schooling. Nevertheless, it is relatively easy to list some key features of higher order thinking. When we do this, we become aware that, although we cannot define it exactly, we can recognize higher order thinking when it occurs. Consider the following:
>
> 1   Higher order thinking is non-algorithmic. That is, the path of action is not fully specified in advance. Higher order thinking tends to be complex. The total path is not "visible" (mentally speaking) from any single vantage point.
> 2   Higher order thinking often yields multiple solutions, each with costs and benefits, rather than unique solutions.
> 3   Higher order thinking involves nuanced judgment and interpretation.
> 4   Higher order thinking involves the application of multiple criteria, which sometimes conflict with one another.
> 5   Higher order thinking often involves uncertainty. Not everything that bears on the task at hand is known.
> 6   Higher order thinking involves self-regulation of the thinking process. We do not recognize higher order thinking in an individual when someone else "calls the plays" at every step.
> 7   Higher order thinking involves imposing meaning, finding structure in apparent disorder.
> 8   Higher order thinking is effortful. There is considerable mental work involved in the kinds of elaborations and judgments required.[xi]

Resnick might have been referring to thinking as something that individuals do when she wrote this but her description could equally apply to the qualities of thoughtful and creative dialogues.

Why it is possible to teach thinking

In a section above I introduced the criticism of the whole idea of teaching thinking because thinking does not exist on its own but is always thinking about something. The critics of teaching thinking are clearly not right because there is good evidence that we can teach thinking; however, their argument is useful because it makes us question a misguided assumption about thinking. If we look at the evidence it shows that programmes that treat thinking as some kind of clearly defined thing (e.g. teaching formal logic) do not work, while the programmes that work best all emphasize the quality of human relationships and promote real dialogue. This evidence suggests that the critics of teaching thinking are quite right that 'thinking' is not some sort of object or thing or content area that can be taught and learnt about, it is more like a relationship. That is why thinking is 'always about something' or always about someone, because it is bound up with how we relate to each other and to the world around us. Where the critics of teaching thinking have been proved wrong is in imagining that teaching cannot cope with a subject that does not have a content area; in this they reveal the simplistic views that non-teachers often have about teaching. Teaching is never just the transmission of content matter: it is always also the development of attitudes and dispositions and relationships. The fact is that we can, as teachers, improve the quality of the way that people relate to each other and to new challenges and by doing this we can teach better thinking. The child who responds to new people with questions and genuine interest is likely to respond to new ideas in the classroom with the same open curiosity and so is likely to learn more and to think better. When we understand thinking not as some kind of thing but as a kind of relationship – a way of responding to that which is 'other' and that which is 'new' – then it is easy to see how it is possible to teach for 'general thinking skills' that will help in every context of life. Of course there might be a few more details to this or I would not have written a whole book about it but in essence a dialogic approach to teaching for thinking and creativity is summed up by encouraging children to be open and to ask questions.

Some evidence that teaching thinking works

There have been many evaluations of teaching thinking programmes over the years and their findings can give us an insight into what works and what does not work. Extensive evaluations going all the way back to Thorndike in 1913 have failed to find much evidence for general thinking skills being developed by programmes focusing on formal thinking either through teaching Latin grammar, formal logic or mathematics. A more recent example of this was the evaluation of the use of LOGO, a logical computer programming language, which is used in many schools. The computer metaphor of mind I outlined above characterizes good thinking as logical thinking and so learning logical thinking by programming computers was expected to lead to generally improved thinking even in other areas. However, evaluations of the impact of engagement in LOGO programming did not find this effect. There was an exception to this; where LOGO was used to encourage small groups of children to talk together and solve problems together and where teachers explicitly helped the children apply the same principles to other problems, then some evidence for the development of general thinking skills was found.[xii]

1 Cognitive Acceleration through Science Education

CASE (Cognitive Acceleration through Science Education) is one of the most successful and well-evaluated programmes in the UK. CASE succeeded in raising pupils' grades in GCSE examinations (on average one grade) two to three years after the programme had been completed.[xiii] Some claim that CASE is based on a Piagetian view of how we learn to think which I have described above as rather mechanistic and not very dialogic. But if we focus on how Piaget is used within the CASE approach we see that the sort of problems Piaget used to separate the operational thinkers (early stage) from what he called formal thinkers (more advanced) were used as problems which were discussed and solved together by groups of children. A classic example of this is the conservation problem whereby the same amount of water is put into two beakers, one thin and one fat, and the children are asked which has more water: the operational stage children are supposed to say that there is more water in the thin beaker because it is taller but the formal stage children say they are both the same. In CASE this task and similar tasks that had been used by Piaget as tests to distinguish one stage of cognitive development from another, was used as a problem to be solved by getting children to talk and think together about it.[xiv] This is a brilliant move that succeeds in teaching thinking by engaging children in critical and creative dialogue to solve problems together in a way that fits better with the metaphor of thinking as dialogue than it does with the metaphor of thinking as a complex mechanism.

2 Thinking Together

In the Thinking Together approach, which I say more about in the next chapter, a series of Talk Lessons are followed, in which classes establish ground rules for collaboration such as listening with respect, responding to challenges with reasons, encouraging partners to give their views and trying to reach agreement. These activities are not only concerned with improving the quality of children's working relationships, but also with developing their use of language as a tool for reasoning and constructing knowledge.

A control study found significant gains in scores on curriculum tests in science and mathematics when this approach was used for a year. Several studies in the UK and Mexico have found significant improvements in solving reasoning test problems when working together in small groups.[xv] Video analysis has demonstrated a link between solving such problems and the use of Exploratory Talk.[xvi] This effect also transferred to significant improvements in individual scores on standard reasoning tests. This programme was developed using the thinking as cultural tool use metaphor in which a way of using words, Exploratory Talk, was said to be a kind of cultural tool to support thinking. This is not false but it does not really explain exactly how children solved new problems together. In the next chapter I will give examples to show why this research supports an understanding of teaching thinking as induction into dialogue.

3 Philosophy for Children

Philosophy for Children is possibly the most positively evaluated thinking skills programme. A stimulus such as a story or picture is shared and pupils are encouraged to think more deeply through a community approach to 'enquiry' in the classroom. This involves teachers developing open-ended Socratic questioning, challenging the children to think more independently and to engage in teacher–pupil and pupil–pupil reciprocal dialogue. One recent large scale evaluation study found evidence of significant gains in a broadly ranged cognitive abilities test. Sessions were held weekly over 16 months with pupils aged 10 and 11. Improved outcomes occurred in a way that was not dependent on the school, the social class of the children or their gender, and which showed the biggest effect for pupils of middle ability. There was also evidence from the study to indicate that classroom behaviour improved and that the pupils' self-esteem and confidence rose. Pupils' participation in classroom discussion increased and they tended to provide more rational underpinning for their opinions. Pupils, it is claimed, also became more aware of their own feelings and those of others.[xvii]

The success of Philosophy for Children is interesting because it exemplifies a dialogic approach. It works by encouraging and supporting real dialogues, understood as shared enquiries into meaning, in classrooms. Almost regardless of what the dialogues are about the children learn to think better and do better on a wide range of tests. More importantly they engage more in education and take more responsibility for their own lives. Philosophy for Children is particularly good at developing the capacity to ask interesting questions.

How to teach for thinking

In this chapter I have discussed arguments about thinking and the possibility of teaching thinking from the disciplines of psychology and philosophy. These are interesting but the best evidence and arguments come from the discipline of education itself. Research evidence in education shows quite clearly that engaging children in interactive or 'dialogic' talk is the best way to teach for cognitive development.[xviii] In education we know that it is possible to teach for thinking and we know which approaches work and which do not. My dialogic theory of thinking and teaching for thinking comes out of this evidence but it also helps us understand educational practice. According to evaluations, the Philosophy for Children approach is a good way to teach for thinking; it is also the approach that most centrally exemplifies the claim that thinking is dialogic and that learning to think is about drawing children into complex and meaningful dialogues.

The basic approach of Philosophy for Children is very simple and can be applied in all curriculum areas. It is particularly easy to adapt to creative writing in English but could also be used to discuss issues in science or in any other subject. It is a good idea to set up some rules initially for talking together such as listening with respect to others and following on from previous ideas (I say more about ground rules for talk in the next chapter). Chairs or cushions are then usually set in a circle and a stimulus is shared. This could be a story, a poem, a picture or anything at all that might prompt thinking. Picture books for young children are often particularly powerful sources for creative thinking. I was impressed with the quality of thinking generated in one classroom by reading *Where the Wild Things Are* together.[xix] The participants are then asked to think of what is strange, interesting or unusual about the stimulus and share their thoughts about this with a partner before coming up with some questions. These questions are written on a board, discussed together and the starting question is chosen. One good way of choosing the question is by 'omni-voting' where each participant can vote as many times as they like and the class vote in turn for each question with one child keeping the score. In the following discussion children are asked to respond, sitting in a circle, building on each other's ideas, with the teacher probing for reasons, examples and alternative viewpoints. At the end of the session the discussion is reviewed and comments are invited from the participants to reflect on the discussion, making links to real situations and possible extra work.

Although this approach is called Philosophy for Children it can be used at any age from reception class onwards. I have used it successfully with mature research students discussing different ideas and approaches in educational research.

A key part of the Philosophy for Children method is moving discussions from the factual level of what things are there, towards 'why' and 'how' and 'what if' questions. Although the technique is quite simple, this role of the teacher as a facilitator for the emergence of more conceptual thinking is not always easy and training is probably a good idea. Training in Philosophy for Children aims to give teachers strategies to manage children's dialogues and to model the sort of language that supports reflection. Some of the kinds of questions a teacher uses, and encourages the children to use, reveal the 'thinking skills' that are being modelled:

- Open questions. (What don't we understand here? What questions do we have?)
- Hypotheses. (Does anyone have any alternative suggestions or explanations?)
- Reasons. (What reasons are there for doing that? Or evidence for believing this?)
- Examples. (Can anyone think of an example of this? Or a counter example?)
- Distinctions. (Can we make a distinction here? Or give a definition?)
- Connections. (Is anyone able to build on that idea? Or link it with another?)
- Implications. (What assumptions lie behind this? What consequences does it lead to?)
- Intentions. (Is that what was really meant? Is that what we are really saying?)
- Criteria. (What makes that an example of X? What really counts here?)
- Consistency. (Does that conclusion follow? Are these principles or views consistent?)[xx]

The model questions suggested in the parentheses above are used by the teacher to guide the children to appropriate this kind of questioning for themselves. Getting the children or students to ask questions themselves is a key part of Philosophy for Children. It is a good idea to use the construction together of good questions as a basis for small group work before discussing in a whole class or whole group circle. For example, after the stimulus, ask individuals to come up with two good questions, then form pairs and argue about which questions are the best ending up eliminating two questions and keeping two questions. These two questions are then taken forward to groups of four children and again the aim is to eliminate two and keep two. Finally the remaining questions are put on a whiteboard and the whole group votes as to which one to discuss first.

The idea expressed in Philosophy for Children training manuals of the importance of moving children towards conceptual thinking is shared by Piaget and the cognitive tradition discussed above. However, concepts have sometimes been seen as overarching categories of a mathematical kind. For example, in mathematics the concept of a triangle is said to include all the particular kinds of triangle in the world, be that a right angle triangle, an equilateral triangle or an isosceles triangle. This is not the kind of thinking we normally see in Philosophy for Children sessions. If we look at how children really talk and think together we find that the questions asked deepen the dialogue by exploring key distinctions and widen the dialogue by bringing in alternative ways of seeing issues. Through such questions, spaces of reflection are created in which ideas resonate with each other and new ideas emerge. These are never the only 'correct' ideas, like finding the right overarching concept; instead each new idea is a new metaphorical way of seeing things amongst others. A story about a boy being naughty, for example, might be seen in the light of not breaking important rules (one point of view) or it might be seen in the light of having a bit of fun (another, equally valid, but very different point of view). Philosophy for Children exemplifies dialogic teaching and learning because it is about teaching questioning and teaching dialogue. Through improving the quality of their questioning and the quality of their dialogue the participants improve the quality of their thinking.

Once I recorded and analysed several sessions of Philosophy with young children, only 5 and 6-years-old. It was striking how, in the first session, they did not know how to engage in dialogue at all but seemed to talk only as individuals. Each one said their own thing regardless of what others were saying, not even noticing if what they said contradicted what others had said. By the end of a few sessions, with the guidance of the teacher, they began to link what they said to what had been said before, perhaps agreeing or disagreeing or just offering an idea that was prompted by the preceding idea. As a result of following on from others in this way they began to develop extended trains of thought about each issue in which assumptions were questioned and new ways of seeing the issue were brought in. A similar shift was noticeable in the questions that they asked. In the first session these were mostly factual questions with discrete answers like 'What did Max have for dinner?' or 'What was the name of Max's boat?'. As the sessions progressed the questions became questions of meaning in the story like 'Why was Max naughty?' and even questions of meaning in general like 'What does it mean to be naughty?'. This evident progress in thinking should not be understood as the development of some kind of 'concept' or 'cognitive structure' but as the deepening and widening of a kind of space, specifically what I call 'dialogic space'; the sort of space in which it becomes possible to reflect on ideas and see them from lots of different points of view at once. That space was in the room between the children as they all sat on cushions in a circle with the teacher, but it was also growing in each one of them, carried with them into conversations in the playground and in the way they responded to things that happened to them and the things that they saw. Philosophy for Children is exemplary of dialogic education because it promotes the opening, deepening and widening of dialogue as an end in itself. This is just another way of saying that by the end of a series of Philosophy sessions children know how to ask better questions; the sort of questions that open things up as opposed to the sort of questions that close things down.

Chapter Summary

In this chapter I explain what teaching for thinking and creativity is and how it can be done. I begin with my own experience as a trainee teacher trying to teach for more than just exams but without a very clear idea of what I wanted to do or of how to do it. The teaching for thinking and creativity movement stems from this kind of practical pressure from teachers who want to make a positive difference in young people's lives. However, to teach for thinking and creativity a theory of how to do this is needed and most of the theories available up until now have not been of very much use. In their place I offer a dialogic theory of how we learn to think that explains why some teaching thinking approaches work and others do not. While most theories of thinking try to describe thinking as some kind of external thing, this dialogic theory describes thinking as a response within a relationship. One aim of teaching for thinking and creativity is to promote a more open, curious and questioning relationship to others and to the world. 'Higher order thinking skills', such as creativity, reasoning, evaluating and reflective self-monitoring, all appear to originate in the context of dialogues. By teaching children to engage more effectively in complex and meaningful dialogues with others we are teaching them the essence of thinking.

In the rest of the book I develop a theory of how to teach for thinking and creativity through chapters focusing on the big themes of dialogic, creativity and reason and then give illustrations of how to apply this theory to teaching across the curriculum in chapters on thinking strategies and on ICT use.

2 What is Dialogic Education?

Chapter Overview

The Cambridge Review of Primary Education draws on a vast amount of research evidence to conclude that the quality of classroom talk, particularly interactive talk, is key to children's understanding of the curriculum.[i] The kind of education required to promote understanding is referred to as 'dialogic', but what exactly is dialogic education and how does it work to develop thinking and creativity? This chapter addresses that question.

Dialogic education means teaching *for* dialogue as well as teaching through dialogue. That sounds simple – and is simple – but it also implies a profound change in how we understand education.

The significance of the idea of *dialogic* (as opposed to traditional *logic*) came to me when working in a team with Neil Mercer and Lyn Dawes, trying to teach children to think by getting them to talk together better around computers in primary classrooms.[ii] I had to analyse many videos of children solving problems together looking for what made the difference between successful and unsuccessful groups. I found that the thing that made the most difference was not the 'cognitive strategies' they were using so much as the quality of their relationships. The extent to which they were really 'in dialogue' with each other made a difference to their ability to think together. I called this the dialogic quality of their relationships and found indicators of it in things like a willingness to ask each other to help them understand, openness to a change of opinion in the face of arguments and individuals being able to admit that they had been wrong and someone else had been right.

In this chapter I will begin with a little more background and an illustration of this research showing how the ability to think together better was taught in classrooms. I think that this research provides solid evidence to support the claim that becoming more dialogic is central to learning to think better. Then I will briefly outline a theory as to what *dialogic* really is and why it is so important to thinking and to education. Finally I will give some practical suggestions as to how a dialogic approach can be applied to transform teaching and learning within the curriculum.

Evidence that dialogic education leads to improved thinking

Our research developing the quality of talk around computers was prompted by earlier research which seemed to show that often group work really did not work very well at all. Teachers, when interviewed, claimed that one important reason why they put children together at computers in twos and threes was to help them develop communication skills. However, having set children to work together in pairs or groups at the computer, teachers in primary classrooms usually had no time to observe their interaction as they had to busy themselves with all the other children in the class. The research team used static cameras on stands near the computers to record everything that happened when the teachers were not there. When these videos were shown to teachers they were often shocked at what they saw. It was common for one dominant child to take charge, positioning himself or herself centrally in front of the screen and grabbing the mouse while the others sat back and watched. When one of the others wanted to have input, there was often fighting over the mouse and over each mouse-click without any constructive dialogue. The best behaved groups sometimes took it in turns to use the mouse and to make decisions but without discussing these decisions with the others so there were no 'communication skills' being developed. Constructive dialogue, where this did occur, was more likely to be about television programmes or about social relationships than about anything related to the educational goals of the activity. Overall the videos showed that children who were asked to work together at computers were confused by the task because they did not yet know how to go about the business of working together effectively. We[iii] responded to this evidence of poor group work by developing an intervention programme to teach them to talk together better. This consisted of a series of lessons both raising their awareness of the impact of the way in which they talked together and also promoting what we called ground rules for effective talk, ground rules like listening with respect and answering challenging questions with reasons instead of either getting angry or ignoring them. Neil Mercer, who was leading the team, called this kind of talk Exploratory Talk to show a link with a tradition of research on talk in classrooms started by Douglas Barnes in the 1970s. Lyn Dawes, an experienced primary teacher as well as an educational researcher, took a lead in developing ten Thinking Together lessons to be taught at least once a week. These focused on developing talk skills and were used in the 'speaking and listening' part of the English curriculum. However, they were also intended as an introduction to a general approach to teaching thinking in every area of the primary curriculum.

At first we tried to assess the effects of our Thinking Together programme on children's talk in small groups around some computer software that I had made called 'Kate's Choice'. This was a story with moral decisions to make. It was easy to see that the amount of talk increased by recording the amount of time spent talking in front of the screens where choices were offered by the computer program. It was also possible to show that the talk after the Thinking Together lessons displayed features of the kind of talk, Exploratory Talk, which we were promoting. We did this simply by transcribing the talk of selected groups in target classes and then counting the number of occurrences of key terms associated with Exploratory Talk like 'because', 'if', 'Why?' and 'maybe'. However, counting that they were using more key words like 'because' did not show that they were really thinking better. How could we show that there was a link between the use of Exploratory Talk and improved thinking?

In response to this challenge we devised the experiment of asking the children in their groups of three to talk about standard reasoning test problems – Raven's non-verbal reasoning tests (see Figure 2.1 below). These kinds of puzzles proved a rich stimulus for talk and they also provided a clear measure of the success or failure of talk as a vehicle for solving problems.

Our talk lessons seemed to work well and after three months of having one lesson a week the children solved more problems correctly than before. This meant that we could compare the same groups of children talking about exactly the same problem three months apart, in the first case failing to solve the problem and in the second case solving it.[iv] These studies comparing successful and unsuccessful talk found that unsuccessful group talk failed in mainly two ways, firstly through the egotism of each individual trying to impose what they saw as their position (we called this disputational talk) and secondly through the stultifying 'group think' effect of individuals uncritically agreeing with each other in order to avoid any disruption to group harmony (we called this cumulative talk). In successful group talk, the most obvious difference was that individuals were able to change their minds, to question their own positions and to ask for help when they did not know the answer. The example below illustrates this difference.[v]

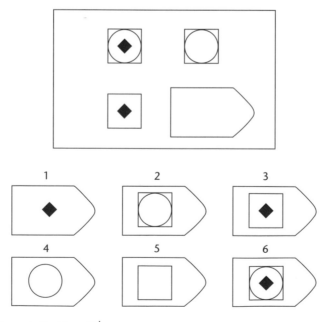

Figure 2.1   Raven's Problem B[vi]

Three short extracts are reproduced here to show the shift towards engaging with each other's thinking.[vii]

Transcript extract 1: Pre-test initiation and challenge

Tara: Square and diamond, it's 2.

Perry: No it's not.

Tara: It is 2.

Perry: No it's not.

Tara: It is.

In the pre-test Tara, a girl, initiates with a suggestion, Perry, a boy, rejects it and they move into a dispute. This disputatious approach continues and eventually Perry imposes his own solution, number 6, against the opposition of two girls, Tara and Keira, by grabbing the pencil and writing down his answer in the space provided.

Transcript extract 2: Post-test initiation and challenge

Tara: That has got to be a diamond, a square with a diamond with a circle in that one, number 6, do you agree?

Perry: No, what do you mean?

Tara: OK, no it's got to be square.

In the post-test, three months later, the same group responds to the same problem quite differently. When Tara suggests number 6 she does so with a question asking if the others agree, Perry then asks her politely to clarify her reasons and, in the act of reflecting on her claim, Tara changes her mind. The talk continues for some time exploring different alternatives. The video also shows long pauses with the group all leaning forwards towards the problem sheet with concentrated expressions. Eventually Tara sees the correct answer and tries to communicate this to the others.

Transcript extract 3: Post-test, sharing the solution

Tara: Look, that's got a triangle, that's got a square. Look, that's got a square with a diamond with a circle in, that's got a square with a diamond in and that's got a square with a circle in so that's got to be a square.

Perry: I don't understand this at all.

Tara: Because, look, on that they've taken the circle out yes? So on that you are going to take the circle out because they have taken the circle out of that one.

Perry: On this they have taken the circle out and on this they have taken the diamond out and on this they have put them both in, so it should be a blank square because look it goes circle square.

After Tara tries to explain her vision, Perry admits that he does not understand her in a way that invites her help. Tara then tries again using the phrase 'taking the circle out'. Perry suddenly seems to see the answer. His eyes light up and he shows signs of excitement. He then repeats Tara's words 'taking the circle out' with energy and animation to express his new understanding.

This illustrates a change that was found more generally. The more successful post-test dialogue contains many examples of children apparently arguing against their own positions, admitting their ignorance, asking for help and changing their minds.

The key change to observe therefore, in the direction of more effective problem solving dialogue, is not only the use of explicit forms of language such as 'because', but the ability of Perry in the post-test to humbly admit that he did not understand, to invite Tara to explain her solution to him and then to adopt her words as his own with pride. In general, across many examples, improvements in the quality of shared thinking are accompanied by children being able to listen to others, change their minds, and argue against their own initial positions.

So how does dialogic education lead to improved thinking?

Our Thinking Together programme is dialogic education since it focuses on teaching children how to learn and think through dialogue and it teaches these skills in a dialogic way, modelling the sort of attitudes and language skills required. But how did this dialogic education work to promote better group thinking? The best way to describe what we observed is in terms of a shift in identity or at least in identification. Identity often refers to things that do not change much like being British or female or a teacher, but there is also a more shifting ground of identifications, like the way in which we might identify with being one kind of person at an office party and then shift to identify with being a different kind of person at a family funeral. Disputational Talk, in which children try to defeat each other and be the winner, depends on an identification with a narrow and defended self-image where what is seen as 'self' is defined against others. This sort of identity can be found in the common phrases 'I win, you lose' or 'winner takes all'. People engaged in Disputational Talk are trying to beat each other, they are not trying to learn from each other. Cumulative Talk, by contrast, depends on all in the group identifying with the group identity more than with their individual identity. They do not want to challenge each other since that might disrupt the harmony of the group. In cumulative thinking there is no incentive to challenge ideas or explore reasoning, instead people seek to agree with each other to maintain the feeling of belonging to the group. We have videos of cumulative groups where different opinions were in fact expressed, almost by accident, but were then just ignored by everyone present in order to maintain the appearance of unity. I expect that we have all been in meetings like that! As well as cumulative and disputational talk we found a third kind of talk which we called Exploratory Talk. When children get carried away in the dialogue, they can challenge the group and even question their own positions. The features of successful problem solving in groups imply a different kind of identity position or temporary identification: this is that of identification, not with any limited image such as self or a group, but with the space of dialogue itself.

The 'space of dialogue' sounds like a vague idea but is simply meant as an answer to the question: from what standpoint are you able to challenge your own thinking? How is it possible for us to change our minds because of what we hear in a discussion? If we are thinking then we are not simply identifying with our initial position or our self-interest, nor are we simply identifying with the other speaker's position, although we are clearly listening carefully. If we are able to change our minds it must be because we are identifying in some way with the process of the dialogue itself and the ideal of truth which it generates.

This account of how group thinking improved in the study suggests a general direction in the development of more effective thinking away from identification with limited entities or images, and towards identification with the space of dialogue. This direction of development is illustrated in Figures 2.2 and 2.3 focusing on the shift that occurred in the Tara and Perry group from Disputational Talk to more dialogic talk.

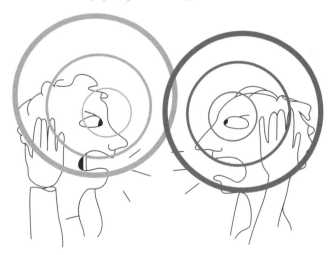

Figure 2.2   Self-identification in dialogue as competition

This illustrates that when engaging more effectively in dialogue the children do not only change the way that they use words, they also change the way in which they relate to each other. Evidence of the important ethical dimension of dialogic identity (that is identifying more with the space of dialogue) was found in the changed atmosphere in the classroom and in reported changes in ways of handling disputes in the playground. But of course, as I will explain in more detail later, becoming more 'open to the other' does not mean becoming the same as the other: in listening to you I do not lose my own perspective. Dialogic is about holding different perspectives together in tension and

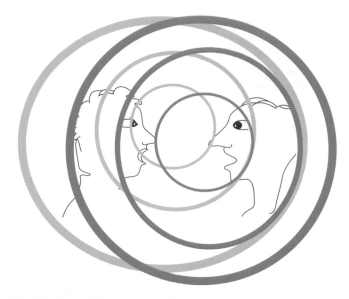

Figure 2.3   Identification with the space of dialogue

inevitably this tension leads to the challenge and competition between ideas which we call *critical* thinking as well as to the spontaneous generation of new ideas and insights which we call *creative* thinking.

Another source for dialogic education

In a fascinating study Robin Alexander[viii] compared talk in primary classrooms in five countries, England, France, India, Russia and the United States. Alexander found a lot of similarities in the use of talk in every country. There was rote, recitation, instruction, exposition and some discussion in every country. However, the kind of talk that he found was most effective for promoting thinking, at the same time as supporting learning, was a kind that he called *dialogue*. He found this kind of talk mostly in Russia where he noticed that teachers would often engage individual pupils in thinking through issues in public by engaging them in long sequences of questions and answers. This inspired him to develop an approach to primary teaching which he calls Dialogic Teaching.[ix]

   In Dialogic Teaching:

1) Questions are carefully framed to encourage reflection and good answers.
2) Answers are not end points but a stimulus for further questions in a long chain of dialogue.
3) The teacher's role is to weave contributions into a coherent whole, leading children to find meaning and helping them think of further questions.[x]

I will say more about how this can be implemented at the end of the chapter, but we can see already that Dialogic Teaching shares many features with the Philosophy for Children approach described in Chapter 1 and the Thinking Together approach introduced above: all three approaches focus on engaging children in live online dialogue as a way of drawing them into thinking and learning.

Evaluations of dialogic education

There have now been quite a few studies on similar lines to the research described above using the Thinking Together approach and evaluating its impact using Raven's tests both in the UK and in Mexico.[xi] These have confirmed not only that teaching Exploratory Talk can help children improve their solving of reasoning tests in groups but also that it appears to increase individual scores on reasoning tests. There have been very similar findings for similar kinds of evaluations of other essentially dialogic approaches such as Philosophy for Children[xii] which also encourage children to become more reflective and able to listen to each other and reason together. Alexander's approach to dialogic teaching has been intensively trialled in London, Yorkshire and other parts of Britain, and due to its success in promoting thinking, as well as learning, it is now incorporated into professional support material from the Quality Curriculum Agency and the UK government's Primary and Key Stage 3 strategies.

So why the term 'dialogic'?

I have referred to two sources of dialogic education in UK primary schools and to evidence that dialogic education works to promote learning in a way that also promotes creative and critical thinking, but what exactly does this word 'dialogic' mean and where does it come from? Some claim that dialogic education is just a return to the focus on group work and collaborative learning that could be seen in UK primary education in the 1970s and 1980s. I think this shows a widespread confusion of dialogic with the everyday use of the word dialogue. This is understandable since most dictionaries define dialogic as simply 'pertaining to dialogue'. However, if you think about the example with which I started this chapter you can see that this is not enough. Both the unsuccessful talk and the successful talk of the children could be called 'dialogues' but the more successful talk was, I claimed, more dialogic.

Robin Alexander often refers to Russian philosopher Michael Bakhtin (1875 to 1975) as the source of his use of the term 'dialogic'. In particular he refers to Bakhtin's contrast between dialogue and conversation. Dialogue, for Bakhtin, is *shared enquiry* in which answers give rise to further questions forming a continuous chain of questions and answers.[xiii]

'Dia' comes from a Greek word meaning 'through' or 'across' and 'logic' from a Greek word meaning speech but also used to refer to reason, so 'dialogic' means literally 'reason across difference'. Bakhtin pointed out that what we had been calling 'logic' and mistaking for reason itself, was really just 'monologic'. The tradition of thinking as logic says that good reasoning is about following rules mechanically to reduce apparent differences to identity. The essential principle of this kind of logic is called the principle of identity, that a thing is what it is and not another thing, or $A = A$.[xiv] In reality, Bakhtin pointed out, people do not normally think like this at all. We think in dialogues where what we say or write responds to what other people have said or written so there is always more than one voice and more than one way of seeing things. Only the systematic thinking of computers is really monologic, human thinking is always bursting with the surprising creativity that comes from holding multiple voices together in the tension of dialogue.

Bakhtin described several ways in which writing and talking can be located on a monologic to dialogic continuum. For example, he wrote that texts can be more or less multi-voiced and that they can be more or less 'open to the other'. He distinguishes, for example, between the 'authoritative' (more monologic) voice that remains outside my own words and the 'internally persuasive' (more dialogic) voice that enters inside my words. Think, for example, of a notice saying 'No smoking': you either accept this or you reject it but it does not encourage you to reflect. By contrast, a friend trying to persuade you to give up smoking will try to find words that mean something to you, possibly even taking on your own vocabulary and concerns. Bakhtin's account of the impact of what he called 'the persuasive word' has obvious significance for teaching:

> Such a word awakens new and independent words, organises masses of our words from within and does not remain in an isolated and static condition: it is not finite but open; in each of the new contents that dialogise it, this discourse is able to reveal ever new ways to mean.[xv]

Persuasive words cross the boundary of the self and enter into our world, stimulating our own answering words and so helping us to think. In fact it is this play of words, voices and ways of seeing that really is thinking: not the kind of rigorous formal logic that can be programmed on a computer. Education in general is only possible if words and voices can cross the boundary of the self so that students can learn to speak in new ways and to see things in new ways. Just telling children what they are supposed to learn does not work well in education as the words used remain outside them. They might nod their heads to agree with them and even memorize them in order to repeat them word for word in a test. But their own thoughts are not stimulated and so the words never become their own words able to express something that they understand for themselves.

A dialogic relationship is different from an external relationship because in a dialogic relationship each person is inside the other. It is a sort of 'inside out, outside in' kind of relationship. This can be understood easily if you think about where an utterance in a dialogue starts. If my son Danny and I are playing with Lego and he shows me a Roman catapult he has made and I say: 'That is pretty cool, but I think it needs something: let's try putting a bar here to stop the arm going too far,' you might think it is obvious that the utterance starts with me saying, 'That is pretty cool,' but even as I framed that utterance my image of Danny was there on the inside because I was speaking for him. The words 'That is pretty cool' came quite naturally but I would not say that if my boss, the Vice-Chancellor of Exeter University, showed me his latest report on how the university is going to reach its research targets. In other words, I naturally use Danny's vocabulary and style because I am responding to him. In any dialogue the person you are speaking to, the 'addressee', is always already there at the beginning of the utterance just as you are there in their heads, so to speak, when they reply to you. In any dialogue we do not just address ourselves to the other person but to our idea of them, which includes our idea of how they are likely to respond to what we are saying. Sometimes this complexity resembles the lines of a popular song which begins: 'I know that you know, that I know that you know, that ....'. This difference between external relations between things and the much more complex internal dialogic relations between people is illustrated in the contrast between Figure 2.4 ('thunk') and Figure 2.5 ('think'):

Figure 2.4   External relations (thunk)

Figure 2.5   Dialogic relations (think)

Real education, education that leads children to think for themselves, depends upon the persuasive word described by Bakhtin and on the dialogic relations illustrated in Figure 2.5. Real education is not about transmitting information and using questions to check if the student received it, but it is about using questions to stimulate answering words and insights and understandings in students. As both the Rose Review of the Primary Curriculum and the Cambridge Review of Education stress,[xvi] real education is about understanding ideas, not just learning how to repeat them, and understanding requires dialogic relations. Dialogic relationships of shared enquiry leading to understanding are central to the approach called Thinking Together developed by Neil Mercer, Lyn Dawes and myself, and also in the Dialogic Teaching approach developed by Robin Alexander. That is why both approaches can be taken to exemplify dialogic education.

Why human thinking is essentially dialogic: A view from psychology

Having established that dialogic relations are crucial to education for understanding I could stop there and go on to give some more ideas for a dialogic approach to education. But I want to understand why and how dialogic works to open up creative thinking. As I outlined in Chapter 1, compared to some of the traditions for understanding thinking, the idea that thinking is essentially dialogic seems strange. In the classic cognitive psychology tradition, for example, thinking has generally been understood to be a kind of mechanical operation of the kind done by computers and so teaching general higher order thinking skills can be seen in terms of programming the mind (or the 'central processor' as the mind is often called in this tradition) with more efficient cognitive and meta-cognitive strategies.[xvii]

However, against this classic cognitive account of thinking and learning to think, there is increasing evidence from developmental psychology that children learn to think creatively through first establishing loving relationships. Peter Hobson, for example, offers experimental evidence for his argument that an initial dialogic relationship between infant and mother (or other primary care-giver presumably) is essential to learning to think because only this relationship enables children to see things from two perspectives at once. Figure 2.6 shows how this works in detail. The first obvious sign we all learn to use is a simple pointing finger showing us where to look. The mother smiles and says, 'Look!' and points at a new toy. The baby looks at her eyes and her pointing finger in order to follow the direction she indicates and so sees the new toy. Soon the baby learns to point at things and to get her mother to look at them.

In order to understand the sign of pointing the baby has to take the perspective of her mother in imagination. Seeing things from two perspectives at once is what makes thinking and using signs possible in the first place.[xviii] For example, when an infant sees a toy that makes them nervous, a robot saying 'What is your name?' for example, they will immediately turn to their mother and see what reaction she has to the same toy. If she smiles and laughs then they may pick it up but they do so now with two perspectives in mind, their own initial reaction and that of their mother. Later, and this is the significance of the curved dotted line in the triangle in Figure 2.6, they learn that by taking a different perspective, the perspective of another person, they can create symbols, using one thing to stand for another, a piece of paper for a doll's blanket perhaps. Such a play symbol is one thing from the adult world perspective, a piece of paper, and another thing for the doll in this case, a blanket. Hobson claims that early dialogic relationships in which we learn to see from two perspectives, beginning with smiles and peek-a-boo games, are the origin of creative thought because they open up 'mental space', a space of possibilities through which things become thinkable and bits of the world can be turned into signs and symbols for thinking about the rest of the world.

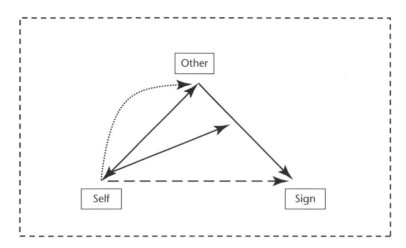

Figure 2.6 The Self-Other Sign triangle from Hobson

Thinking, on this dialogic account, is essentially a process of taking multiple perspectives. This is a skill which has to be learnt initially in close relationships (later, as we will see more in Chapter 5, it can be practised alone).

Hobson directly related his account of the importance of the relationship with the mother (or other primary care-giver) in the early years to the development of general thinking skills when, working with colleagues, he devised an experiment demonstrating a correlation between the quality of the dialogic relation between toddlers at 3 years and their mothers and their IQ scores.[xix]

Hobson is not alone in his arguments that thinking and learning to think are essentially dialogic. Tomasello and colleagues contrasted normal human development to that of the great apes.[xx] Apes, they claim, can learn to see others as agents with intentionality but cannot develop a truly dialogic relation with others. Human children, by contrast to apes, have, they claim: 'a species-unique motivation to share emotions, experience, and activities with other persons'. The result of this is, they argue, the development of the ability to engage in shared intentionality, which, following Hobson, I interpret as the ability to see things through other people's eyes as well as through their own. This skill enables human children to participate in culture and shared thinking.

Tomasello and his team of researchers at the Max Planck Institute in Germany are at the cutting edge of research on how human thinking emerged from ape cognition.

They specifically take on and reject the widespread argument that it is the internalization of language use that develops creative human thinking, writing:

> What could it mean to say that language is responsible for understanding and sharing intentions, when in fact the idea of linguistic communication without these underlying skills is incoherent. And so, while it is true that language represents a major difference between humans and other primates, we believe that it actually derives from the uniquely human abilities to read and share intentions with other people.[xxi]

This quote is really important for me because it neatly shows why a dialogic perspective on education goes beyond a Vygotskian 'socio-cultural' perspective.[xxii] Vygotsky is often referred to as claiming that we learn to think by internalizing language and other cultural tools. Of course language and cultural tools are important for the specific ways in which we learn to think in different places and times but before language use there are relationships. Thinking does not start with words, it starts with a baby seeing things as if from her mother's point of view and the mother seeing things as if from the baby's point of view. And beyond language and tools there is also always relationship. Feeling the pain or the joy of another person and understanding them through this does not depend on words but on something deeper than words and bigger than words.

Hobson and Tomasello are not alone in their account of the importance of dialogic engagement to the development of thinking. A review of the literature suggests that the discovery of the importance of dialogic relationships to early cognitive development has the force of an emerging consensus in psychology.[xxiii]

Why human thinking is essentially dialogic: A view from philosophy

The two disciplines that most closely concern themselves with understanding thinking are psychology and philosophy. As a science, psychology tends to approach thinking from the outside as something to be defined, measured and explained.[xxiv] Some schools of philosophy have taken the opposite tack and tried to understand thinking from the inside in the very act of thinking. The school of phenomenology, for example, founded by Edmund Husserl at the end of the nineteenth century sought to return to things 'as they appear to us'. While Husserl himself described thinking solely in terms of the actions of a self or ego, those influenced by him, particularly his best student and his successor at the University of Freiburg, Martin Heidegger, described thinking in terms that are more dialogic. I mentioned Heidegger briefly in Chapter 1 and I will say more about his account of teaching and learning thinking in the next chapter, Chapter 3, but here I just want to draw attention to the dialogic nature of thinking that he uncovered and how this was taken up.

In his important work 'Was heisst Denken?' sometimes translated as 'What calls thinking?' Heidegger begins with the claim: 'We come to know what it means to think when we ourselves are thinking. If our attempt is to be successful, we must be ready to learn thinking.'[xxv] Thinking has to be learnt, he writes, but the first step in learning thinking must be to unlearn all the nonsense that has been taught about thinking. He writes, for example, that 'Science is not thinking'. He means here that accounts of thinking (and science) as facts linked by neat convincing logical arguments are at best accounts of thinking made up after the event that tell us nothing about what thinking is really like. So what is thinking really like, then? Heidegger does not answer this question directly but he replaces it with another question: 'What calls us to think?'[xxvi] By doing this he is pointing out that while science describes thinking as if it was a process that we can control, like applying a method of argument, the actual experience is much more like being called to think by something beyond us. He writes, rather obviously perhaps, that what most calls us to think is that which we find most thought provoking. In other words we are called to think by something which we sense is really important, but which we cannot grasp, so we end up running after it without ever quite catching up with it. Using rather poetic language, he writes of that which calls us to think as creating a wind or a draught as it withdraws from us, so that thinking should be understood as like being drawn into this draught. While we can never fully grasp hold of that which calls us to think, the very fact that we allow ourselves to be called by it means that our thinking becomes a kind of pointing towards it.

Levinas, another phenomenologist, was at first a keen student of Heidegger. Levinas was Jewish however and lost most of his family in the Holocaust. Heidegger, meanwhile, took up a position of rank within the Nazi party. After the war it is perhaps not surprising that Levinas became a fierce critic of Heidegger, but he still had a Heideggerian way of thinking. Levinas attacked Heidegger's ethics pointing out something striking: there was no mention of the importance of other people in Heidegger, or at least never in a positive way. Heidegger wrote at length about our relationship with 'Being' but never about our relationship to other people, except to criticize our tendency to conform to the conventional thinking of the masses. Levinas accepted Heidegger's claim that we are called out to think by something beyond us but this 'something' is not, he claimed, a mysterious abstraction like 'Being', as Heidegger had implied. What calls us to think, Levinas said, is really the face of another human being. Thinking begins, Levinas claims, when we are called to explain ourselves in the face of real other people. From the very beginning, to be a self, for Levinas, is to be a kind of response to others who call us out: they call 'Are you there?' and the self says 'Here I am' ('me voici').[xxvii] It is in the context of a relationship of responsibility (a need to respond) binding us to other people that we are called to think in order to justify and explain ourselves to others.

Levinas's account of how thinking is called out within the context of relationship links back clearly to Hobson's image of the infant in the arms of its mother responding to her face. But although Levinas writes a lot about concrete real other people, his account of thinking is not really all that different from his teacher Heidegger's original account. He writes that there is something about other people that we can never grasp, their 'absolute otherness' from us, and it is this mysterious and ungraspable Otherness of the other that is what most calls out to us.

The description of thinking as a kind of response to the call of Being for Heidegger or as a response to the call of Otherness for Levinas, can be called dialogic not because it locates all thinking in real dialogues between specific individuals but because it assumes that thinking is a flow across difference that requires at least two poles to get it going. Real thinking, they are saying, is not at all like the story that has been told by cognitive scientists, it is not at all like playing a reasoning game on one's own according to logical rules. It is much more like an unpredictable and uncontrollable flow of sparks of insight arcing out from one electric pole to another.

Applying dialogic education in the classroom

Dialogic education means teaching in a way that draws children into thinking by drawing them into dialogue. Anything can be taught in a way that frees children to think at the same time as they learn. In particular the Thinking Together programme I began this chapter with, explicitly focuses on teaching for dialogue, giving children the skills and the confidence to effectively think and learn together with others. This Thinking Together approach developed several lesson plans and activity ideas for creating a talking and thinking atmosphere in the classroom.[xxviii] We developed the following 'ground rules' partly influenced by a survey of the literature on effective collaborative learning, but mainly from our experience in classrooms:

- all relevant information is shared.
- the group seeks to reach agreement.
- the group takes responsibility for decisions.
- reasons are expected.
- challenges are acceptable.
- alternatives are discussed before a decision is taken.
- all in the group are encouraged to speak by other group members.

The Thinking Together website provides resources including lessons that establish some important ideas about talk and lead children to devise a set of ground rules as near to our own as possible. We found it helps if these rules are converted into a clear and simple version, which the children can appreciate and follow. It is vital that each class feels a sense of ownership of, and commitment to, their own set of ground rules. One example from a class I worked with was as follows:

Our talking rules

Everyone should have a chance to talk
Everyone should be listened to carefully
Everyone should be asked:

> What do you think?
> Why do you think that?

Look and listen to the person talking
After discussion the group should agree on a group idea

Research over the years has found that the success of the Thinking Together approach depends on the teacher's commitment and how they themselves embody the approach in the way that they interact with children. How the teacher models thinking is crucial.[xxix] This is also true of the dialogic teaching approach in which dialogue is used to find out what children think, engage with their developing ideas and help them to talk through misunderstandings. When children are given opportunities to contribute to extended classroom dialogue they can explore the limits of their own understanding. At the same time they can practise new ways of using language as a tool for thinking and learning.

We found that effective teachers:

- reminded children to used the ground rules for talk once they were established, and often used talking partners and small groups so that questions and ideas are talked over.
- 'modelled' the kinds of language they wished to hear. For example, teachers used the whole class sessions to ask 'Why?' and 'How?' questions which provided examples of how this can help make thinking explicit to others.
- used questions not just to test children on specific items of knowledge, but used a series of related questions to lead the class through a line of reasoning. This 'guided reporting' is a common feature of classrooms; it means that the teacher elicits a response from a child, then asks others to build on this contribution in a way that helps the entire class to come to a joint understanding of a topic. This way of provoking discussion through targeted questioning and active listening is a strategy children can usefully learn and subsequently offer to one another when working without teacher support in a small group.
- helped children to recognize and value the language and reasoning skills they are developing. For example, children can consider whether using the ground rules is changing how they talk and work together; and what benefits they perceive.[xxx]

Lyn Dawes[xxxi] gives much further useful guidance for dialogic teaching in practice. Encouraging classroom talk, she writes, can be difficult. Children may not listen to each other and while some children may refuse to engage, others may be too aggressive in challenging. Planning for talk can help overcome these problems. She suggests:

- using plenaries to analyse the talk that has gone on in any activity, asking children to evaluate its quality and impact.
- another technique is to have a 'dialogue star'. 'Choose a child who is expected to make the initial contribution and change every week so each child in class eventually takes this role.'
- in preparing activities plan for 'Why?', 'How?' or 'What do you think?' questions to help start up dialogue.

These principles and guidelines for teaching from the Thinking Together approach are highly compatible with those coming from Alexander's Dialogic Teaching approach. Sylvia Wolfe worked with Robin Alexander to develop a list of strategies through which educationally productive streams of dialogue appeared to be triggered. These include:

- asking real questions.
- pausing to allow children time to i) think and ii) respond in order to express ideas more fully.
- using words such as 'perhaps' and 'might' as invitation to a range of possible actions.
- developing a line of argument with one child through a sequence of connected questions.
- accepting responses without evaluating them.
- engineering opportunities for students to participate actively in talk in the classroom.
- building on children's interests.
- providing opportunities for children to ask questions and make statements.

According to Wolfe these teaching strategies presuppose the existence of at least some of the following features of classroom life:

- teachers have a good knowledge of curriculum content and understanding of the issues that are likely to confuse children or challenge their thinking.
- teachers' questions match the instructional purpose. Some questions will invoke a range of responses and encourage divergent thinking, others will require only single word responses. In the chaining of question and answers ideas are developed or changed.
- teachers encourage learning talk through activities that require children to respond in extended utterances. They model language that goes beyond what learners are able to produce alone.
- teachers listen and respond to the content of students' utterances, challenging, probing and extending their meanings.
- children are offered constructive and formative feedback on performance.
- parties to the dialogues in the classroom are comfortable living with provisionality and uncertainty.
- children can initiate in dialogue and at times the teacher withdraws from the floor.
- students are sometimes expected to address the whole class in an intelligible and articulate way and to listen carefully to each other's contributions.[xxxii]

Conclusions

In Chapter 1 I pointed out that evaluations of thinking skills programmes tend to show that those based on speaking and listening in the context of real dialogues work the best; programmes such as Philosophy for Children and Thinking Together. In this chapter I focused on the development of the Thinking Together approach, which I worked on with Neil Mercer and Lyn Dawes. I also referred to the Dialogic Teaching approach developed by Robin Alexander. Both seem to lead to similar guidelines for practice. The success of both in promoting thinking can be explained by the same dialogic theory.

Thinking skills are often seen as the property of individuals, so the question might be asked, how does engaging in dialogue with others influence the development of individual thinking skills? The evidence from developmental psychology quoted in this chapter increasingly suggests that we learn to think for ourselves by first being drawn into dialogues with others. In dialogue with parents, even in non-verbal peek-a-boo games, young children learn that things can be seen in different ways from different perspectives. To learn something new, even to understand a sign as simple as a mother pointing at a teddy bear, is to be drawn into taking the perspective of another person. Once a child can take the perspective of another person that child is ready to learn anything. Listening to the perspective of another person in a dialogue is never simply passive. As Bakhtin pointed out, really listening to someone else always involves generating our own answering words. So listening is already a kind of speaking. It is also true that speaking, in a dialogue at least, is already a kind of listening because it is necessary to take on the perspective of those we are talking with in order to shape our words to speak to them.

Most important learning is creative in that it requires a leap to see things in a new way. It is hard to understand how this is possible until we see people getting 'carried away' and 'drawn out of themselves' when talking together with others. In dialogues people often find themselves saying things that, before the dialogue, they did not yet know that they knew. It is in this active response to the voices of others that the experience of understanding occurs. This is why dialogic education has to be at the heart of education for understanding.

By teaching children to engage more effectively in dialogues with others (and with otherness in general) we are teaching the most general thinking and learning skill of all. So called 'higher order thinking skills', skills such as creativity, reasoning, evaluating and reflective self-monitoring, all appear to originate in, and to be continuously practised in, the context of meaningful dialogues. One of the most general and useful 'thinking skills' is the skill of being able to suspend all worry about identity – I mean all concern about who I am, who you are and what group we belong to – in order to enter into a creative space of dialogue. Learning to think well is not only about acquiring tools and strategies, although these may help, it is more centrally about becoming more dialogic, which means becoming more open and responsive to others and to new ideas, while also being more comparative, critical and challenging. Becoming more dialogic is also about feeling more at home living in a space of dialogue where there are always many voices and where there is never any certainty.

Chapter Summary

I began this chapter with an account of two young children learning how to solve reasoning test problems together. In the first session they are preoccupied by who is right and who is wrong and so fail to solve the problem. After three months of talk focused teaching they are able to listen to each other, change their minds and humbly ask each other to explain. Of course they can now think better together and they solve the problem that previously was too hard for them. This illustrates that learning to think is not just about acquiring tools, it is also about becoming more dialogic. This means simply having a greater disposition towards engaging in dialogue. In the rest of the chapter I offered ideas from psychology and from philosophy that explain why it is that being drawn into dialogues lies at the heart of thinking and also of creativity. The chapter ended with a number of practical ideas for implementing dialogic education in primary classrooms.

3 Creative talk

Chapter Overview

Teaching for creativity is a recent priority for education around the world. However, the roots of creativity remain obscure. This chapter begins with an account of the importance of collaborative creativity and the discovery of the educational significance of children's playful talk. I argue that creativity originates in the capacity to 'let go' of the self into a shared place of multiple perspectives and possibilities that is found first in playful relationships. The chapter goes on to describe how this space of possibilities can be increased in classrooms and also guided in ways that promote not only creative play but also the creative fashioning of valued ideas and products.

If key words were stocks and you had invested in 'creativity' fifty years ago you would probably be rich by now. When respected educationalist Benjamin Bloom produced a taxonomy of higher order thinking in education in 1956 creativity was not even on his list.[i] But when this same taxonomy was recently revised for a new century by two former students of his, creativity was put top of the list as the very highest of higher order thinking skills.[ii]

Despite the rise in the value given to creativity in education there is still a widespread lack of clarity as to what creativity really is, where it comes from and how best to teach for it. When governments say that they want to promote creativity what they probably really mean is that they want to promote applied creativity leading to successful innovations that make lots of money and preferably also start new industries that employ lots of people. There is often a tension in our use of the term creativity between, on the one hand, a view of creativity as a kind of freedom to play around and, on the other, a focus on ideas that are not only original but also valuable and influential. If asked for examples of creativity most people suggest things like Van Gogh's 'sunflower', Einstein's 'theory of relativity' or Apple's 'iPod', ignoring all the countless pictures, ideas and products that never made it to iconic status. Meanwhile we still say that children mucking around with paint and paper are 'being creative' even if the outcome is of no value and goes into the dustbin (only when the children's attention has moved on, of course, as we don't want to discourage them with adult value judgements!). This same tension can be seen in a definition of creativity produced by a UK government commission on creativity in education. The group defined creativity as: 'Imaginative activity fashioned so as to produce outcomes that are original and of value',[iii] neatly combining in one sentence the two sides of creativity, 'imaginative activity' on one side and social 'value' on the other.

It is clear that in talking about creativity in education the government want to promote the fashioning of valued products. This is one aspect of creativity which I refer to from now on as creativity 2. On the other hand it is not possible to get creativity 2, socially valued products, without first having lots of creativity 1, the everyday creativity of playfully coming up with lots of new and different ideas, connections and ways of seeing things regardless of whether or not these are socially valuable.[iv]

Playful talk in classrooms

One of the first things anyone interested in children's talk in classrooms notices is the great deal of apparently off-task nonsense talk or banter. This does not usually appear in research papers but is just part of the accepted background to school life. Sometimes this way of talking is just annoying, especially when used to avoid focusing on the task set, but it can also turn into really funny and clever improvised humour.

I remember one time when I visited a primary school in a run-down area to record children talking around reasoning tests. I could not get them to focus on the task and they started a spontaneous verbal riff about my car which they had seen coming from the window. 'Mr. Wegerif's car [pause] won't get you very far', a boy said. A girl picked up the rhythm with: 'It's yucky and green'. Someone else chipped in: 'It's a mean machine, a zoomy beam', and so on and so on. The group got more and more excited at their own surreal invention jumping up from their chairs to stand at the window all looking at my car (a truly awful lime green Vauxhall Chevette from a previous generation of car design). After that I struggled to get the class to sit down. When they had calmed down enough to do the tests they did not do very well at all but I left impressed by their verbal creativity.

The research team I was part of at the time was exploring educationally significant talk in classrooms so I discussed this kind of classroom banter with them. Being familiar with schools and classrooms everyone knew exactly the kind of talk I meant. They agreed that this was indeed a type of talk that could be characterized in a similar way to the types of talk that we were working with: types of talk we were calling Disputational Talk, Cumulative Talk and Exploratory Talk.[v] We called this new type of talk Playful Talk and characterized it in terms of a fundamental orientation, not taking anything said seriously, with a concomitant set of ground rules such as 'follow on from the previous speaker but avoid obvious links; the more surprising the continuation the better'. However, although playful talk was discussed by the research team, it was not taken forward into publications or further research plans because we thought of it as off-task talk having no obvious educational value. We were looking for ways of talking that would help them to learn and to think, not to play. Our focus was on Exploratory Talk which we defined through the presence of explicit reasoning such as 'I disagree with you because…'. With hindsight I now think that we were wrong to understand thinking only as reasoning rather than as creativity. As a result of this we could not see the significance of Playful Talk.

With the following four examples of children's talk I want to illustrate the route leading from off-task Playful Talk to more obviously productive classroom talk.

Example 1: Off-task playful talk

It is actually very hard to get children to perform any kind of task at school without their being creative with language. In the following example three 9-year-old children, Sharon, Gail and Nick, were asked to work together around a piece of software called 'Bubble Dialogue'. This software shows cartoon characters in a difficult situation and the users have to fill in the thought bubbles and speech bubbles of the characters. In this case the cartoon characters were called Jane and Robert. Jane knew that Robert had stolen some chocolates from the sweet shop. Now her money was missing and she thought Robert might have stolen that too. Gail, Sharon and Nick were asked to talk together about the issues and think about how the characters would feel. They did not really do that but they did produce some interesting word play. We join them as they construct together what they will type.

Transcript extract 3.1: Funny money

> Sharon: I think
>
> Gail: I think Robert stole the stuff
>
> Sharon: That
>
> Nick: That Robert stole my bunny
>
> (*Sharon and Gail laugh*)
>
> Sharon: My money
>
> Gail: Funny
>
> Nick: It's not money I said bunny
>
> Sharon: It's his money
>
> Gail: I've said bunny

A few lines later they are typing in together the word 'chocolates' and Gail says: 'Lovely, *yummy*, chocolates' echoing the earlier use of money, bunny, and funny. She then continues in a different voice to indicate that she is quoting:

> 'Life is in a box of chocolates'

Nobody picks up this reference to the film *Forest Gump*. Three lines later Gail tries another reference to a different context, singing:

> 'Choc-o-lets. Tasty. Cadbury's Quake'

in the tune of an advertisement for Cadbury's Flake. This time Nick picks this up responding to the use of Quake with the word:

'Quavers'

which is a popular snack also advertised on TV. Sharon, who is typing this whole time, brings them back to the task, as she sees it, by saying:

'Chocolates'

and then beginning to spell it out.

'C, H, O, C'

For now the others join her in spelling out chocolate, but it is not long before the word play breaks out again, 'chocolate' being turned by Sharon into 'choc, then it's late'.

Despite my best efforts these children interpreted the task as more about typing words into the boxes than thinking about issues. What is interesting, though, is that they cannot do this task straight; they rhyme and break into little songs, use silly voices and puns and generally play around with language.

These children are not exceptional. The normality of playful talk has only become apparent in the last decade or so because it has only recently been possible to collect large amounts of ordinary spoken language data for analysis. Before the existence of large amounts of recorded talk research tended to focus more on available written texts. Word play was believed to be a deviant and specifically literary form found in poems. But in fact this creative 'poetic' use of language turns out to be so common in everyday talk amongst equals that it should be considered the norm.[vi]

Example 2: On-task playful talk leading to a product

I am not going to claim that rhyming 'money, bunny, funny and yummy' is in itself something we should call higher order thinking. However, it is creative in one sense in which we normally use the term: that is 'imaginative analogy' or what I am calling creativity 1. For creativity 1 to lead to creativity 2, shared ground rules are important. This is brought out in a transcript extract given originally by Neil Mercer[vii] to illustrate Cumulative Talk, talk in which children share and build on each other's ideas but in an uncritical way. The example he gives is from a session in which two 10-year-old girls, Katie and Anne, were working on the production of their own class newspaper, using some desktop publishing software for schools called *Front Page Extra*. They do not know what to write and Katie starts with 'fun-filled'. Anne likes this and adds a word saying 'fabulous fun-filled' (notice the alliteration).

Transcript extract 3.2: Fantabuloso (from Mercer, 1995)

Katie: Inside these inside these fant, inside these fun-filled, no inside these covers these fantastic these brilliant

Anne: Brilliant

Katie: Is it brilliant?

Anne: No

Katie: No. Fantast fantabuloso shall we put that?

They then repeat the word almost musically to each other, obviously pleased with it: 'fan-tab-ul-oso', says Anne: 'fan-tab-ul-oso-oso' repeats and extends Katie.

Clearly there is no explicit reasoning here so it is clear why Neil Mercer contrasts this to Exploratory Talk, and yet there is implicit judgement going on. Katie and Anne consider various alternatives and reject them. In the little extract above we can see that they are not happy with 'brilliant' and drop it. Fantastic is closer but not quite right so they create a new (for them) hybrid word combining fantastic with fabulous, *fantabuloso*, which is just right for their purposes. If you cannot see this as creative work then just imagine that instead of being children in school they are a couple of creative marketing managers trying to find a new name for a product. Products with very similar names: Fab, Fanta, Brillo etc. already exist and were presumably thought up through a similar kind of shared creative process. The difference between this and the 'money' transcript is that here the talk is oriented to finding the best possible solution to the task set. Sharon, Gail and Nick, in the first example, do not link their verbal play to the task in hand, it is just a bit of fun and if anything it is subverting the task. Their play is creative in that it generates lots of new links and potential ideas – is life really like a box of chocolates? – but they do not build on any of them. Katie and Anne do build on each other's suggestions. They build a new word together, but they do not really think explicitly about it. In the next example we see how a very similar process leads to explicit reasoning of a higher order.

Example 3: On-task playful talk and shared thinking

In this example a teacher I was working with, Mark Prentice, was engaging his class of 8-year-olds in philosophy for children. The children were sitting in a circle on the floor with Mark talking about issues raised by a picture book that they all had in front of them. The book is *Where the Wild Things Are* by Maurice Sendak.[viii] When we join them they have just read aloud about how the hero of the story's bedroom turns into a forest and the bedroom walls 'become the whole world'. The teacher, Mark Prentice, then encourages them to think about imagination and the meaning of the word 'world'. Below is a version of the talk that follows very lightly edited to reduce the length:

Transcript extract 3.3a: Imagining things

Helen: [You can just start] staring at things and make it into your picture. [3 second pause] It can be about twenty things in one place.

Teacher: Say that again Helen because it's interesting.

Helen: There's about twenty things in one place.

Teacher: That you can just look at and stare?

Helen: Yeh, there are also lines on the curtains they could turn into loads of green leaves.

Emma: Yeh, or bamboo stalks.

Teacher: So you can stare at something and get a different picture?

Emma: Yeh, you could change it into a leopard or something.

Teacher: Have you ever done that? Stared at something and looked at all the shapes that are inside it?

Alex: Yeh, you could turn that into a big bone or something.

Teacher: This radiator here – so we have power to change things don't we. How do we do that?

Emma: I was in my room the other day and I closed my eyes nearly shut and my rocking horse I thought it was this kind of a pot – a shaking pot.

I hope you can see how similar this kind of talk is to the talk of Nick, Sharon and Gail in the first extract. Here the children are sharing experiences that resonate with, but are interestingly different from, the experience shared by the previous speaker. Helen can stare at the curtains and turn them into green leaves; Emma says they could also be bamboo shoots or even a leopard. Alex points out that the radiator could be a dinosaur bone and Emma describes how she turned her rocking horse into a 'shaking pot' by squinting at it through half-closed eyes. This is playful talk exhibiting creativity 1, it is thinking together by a sort of resonance of images and ideas, each one triggering the next through something that they have in common. In what happens next the teacher's interventions help to turn this talk into something close to explicit reasoning about the underlying structure of experience.

Transcript extract 3.3b: World creating

Teacher: Can you create your own world?

Several: Yes.

Teacher: How can you create your own world?

Several: Imagining, dreaming.

Teacher: That's interesting so you can create your own world by imagining – did Helen create a world when she started to talk about the curtains up there?

Helen: There's about a thousand worlds all in one person's head, all in one place.

[...]

Teacher: What do you think – Alex?

Alex: Well one time I invented my own country which I called Alexland cos I became my bedroom a whole country and I pretend all my toys are alive.

Teacher: So you created a world.

Alex: Yes.

Teacher: Now is that a real world?

Alex: Well sometimes I feel like it's really real but then when I've found something like a catalogue, which I pretend you couldn't get catalogues and stuff like that, then the world just disappears.

Teacher: So it disappears when you look at something else.

Alex: Yeh, when I look at something – when I go downstairs it just disappears, because my bedroom's the best place – because my toys are up there.

The teacher's role is very important here, he is not giving the group ideas but facilitating group thinking by repeating key points and asking prompting questions.

Here there are few challenges or explicit reasons. Instead the children seem to build on each other's comments with similar experiences and ideas. Helen's idea that things can seem to be different as if 'there were about twenty things in one place' is picked up by Emma and Alex who share examples of this. This is what has been called Cumulative Talk because there is a sharing of experience and ideas without challenges or critical grounding. But it is nonetheless apparent that some serious thinking is going on. This leads to the realization, articulated by Alex, that there can be two different worlds, his own world and the adult world, and that objects from the adult world, found in his world, can make his world dissolve. It could be argued that this is not reasoning but just a description of his experience. However, thinking is implicit in the description. This way of describing experience is a way of seeking to understand it and these descriptions reveal the world in a new way. Alex describes his experience but with insight into its general structure.

This description of how his world can dissolve in the face of anomalous objects is given in response to a prompt by the teacher that could be taken as a challenge 'Is it really real?'. But Alex does not reply to this with any explicit reasoning of the kind 'Yes it is, because' or 'No it isn't, because' – he replies with a description that is also an anecdote:

Well sometimes I feel like it's really real but then when I've found something like a catalogue, which I pretend you couldn't get catalogues and stuff like that, then the world just disappears.

We could say of this that Alex offers a reason why Alexland is not really real. However, the whole utterance here is much more than just a piece of explicit reasoning, it is also a sharing of his experience in a way that invites us inside that experience.

Alex's understanding that one world can be dissolved by the presence of an arte-fact from another world could be seen as a powerful piece of thinking. For me it evokes the role of catalysts in chemistry crystallizing a solution so it turns almost instantly from one thing to another. I also think of the idea of a 'paradigm shift' in science which happens when one 'world view' replaces another sometimes sparked by looking closely at anomalies within the original paradigm.[ix]

My response to what Alex says takes me to new ideas not through explicit reason-ing but through a kind of internal resonance in which the structure of the experience that he articulates opens onto other experiences with a similar structure. It is precisely through this same resonance between perspectives and ways of seeing that the children seem to be building upon each other's ideas. Alex's clear statement of a powerful idea does not come on its own but it emerges within the context of a dialogue between voices – voices that are not just the voices of the children but the voices of texts and TV programmes and moments of experience. This dialogue could just remain descriptive or quirky like the talk of Sharon, Gail and Nick in the first example, rhyming funny with bunny and sharing jingles, but the group are guided by the teacher to reflect on the experience described and find the structure underlying it.

Example 4: Solving a reasoning test problem together

For this example I want to turn back to the example I gave in the last chapter of children solving a reasoning test problem together and think about it again. Success at solving this sort of puzzle, taken from Raven's Standard Progressive Matrices, is a relatively 'hard' measure of thinking ability that correlates well with academic achievement in general. Yet if we look at it closely it is clear that the thinking involved is not algo-rithmic but creative. There is no set of formal procedures that the children can follow to solve this problem, they have to use their imaginations to come up with an answer that fits. Their solution to the problem was expressed in the phrase 'taking the circle out' (see Figure 2.1). But the 2D diagram they have in front of them is static, there is no visible process like 'taking out' that they can point to. This phrase they create to-gether that unlocks the puzzle for them is therefore a metaphor. The process whereby they come up with this metaphor is similar to that of the two girls, Katie and Anne, in Example 2, coming up with the new word, *fantabuloso*. The group tries out many dif-ferent metaphors and ways of seeing the puzzle and decides that each one is not quite right until they find one that is just right because it works to solve the puzzle. But the word *fantabuloso* was not meant to be a thought or a concept, it was just right aestheti-cally for the task rather than conceptually. The phrase 'taking the circle out' is just right for cognitive rather than for aesthetic reasons: it solves the puzzle by revealing the un-derlying structural relationship between the different parts of the diagram. In this way it has similarities with the third example above where Alex, prompted by questions, re-flects on a relationship between his experiences and expresses this in a way that reveals a key structural property of reality change; that a shift in reality always hinges around an anomaly. In both cases open questions prompt reflection on underlying structural properties. When Perry asks Tara 'What do you mean?' she thinks again and changes her proposed solution to the reasoning test, exploring more options. In a similar way when the teacher, Mark Prentice, asks Alex: 'Is it really real?' he responds by exploring his experience and finding that his world sometimes seems real and other times not.

Discussion of these four examples

In presenting these four examples as a series I am, like Alex, making an argument by analogy. In all four cases creativity 1 is the baseline. This is the almost random generation of associations and alternative ways of seeing. In the first example of purely playful talk creativity 1 is an end in itself. Any of the connections made could lead to further development or to deeper thought but they don't, they just lead to laughter and the children move on. The children do not explore why life is like a box of chocolates or why bunny is linked to money; that would not be the point, they are just having fun. In the second example we see similar playful talk coming up with alternative words that fit with their 'fun-filled' theme, words like *fab, fantastic, brilliant*. But this time the play contributes to their task and they construct together a new hybrid word that fits just right: *fantabuloso*.[x] The very fact that it is new to them and not in their dictionary adds to its light and airy evanescent 'fun-filled' feel. The third example illustrates how playful talk is also the baseline and necessary foundation stage for reflection. Again the example starts with the generation of alternative possibilities from experience: a curtain is like leaves, a rocking horse is like a shaking pot, a radiator is like a dinosaur bone. But this playful talk is stimulated and directed by a teacher's questioning trying to get at deeper meaning. One boy, Alex, is led to articulate how his child's reality, 'Alexland', dissolves into an adult reality when an object that only fits in the adult world is encountered in the child world, 'a catalogue or something like that'. Finally we see a similar structure in example 4, solving a reasoning test problem. The almost random generation of alternative ways of solving the puzzle are focused in by reflective open questions until a metaphor embodied in a shared phrase is constructed together: 'taking the circle out'. In the last three examples, *fantabuloso*, reality shift and 'taking the circle out' we can see how creativity 1, imaginative analogy embodied in playful talk, evolves into the beginnings at least of creativity 2, fashioning a valued product. In the case of *fantabuloso* this product is the new word itself, but in the other two cases the words used embody a shared insight into the hidden structure of things. In all cases the shift from creativity 1 to creativity 2 is facilitated by open-ended questions that are focused on the topic: 'Is it "brilliant"?' Katie asks Anne, 'Is it really real?' Mark asks Alex and 'What do you mean?' Perry asks Tara. In each case these reflective questions lead to reflection and the emergence of a better sign or a better explanation.

Creative talk in science

I guess that some readers may not agree with me that fashioning the word '*fantabuloso*' or Alex's account of how his personal play world dissolves, really count as creative products of the kind that we want to promote in education. That is why I included the reasoning test example to show its similarity. There is also good research evidence that very similar creative talk processes lie behind breakthroughs in science that are valued and are crucial for the knowledge economy. Psychologist Kevin Dunbar researched creativity in the area of microbiology by taking his video camera to record conversations in leading laboratories. In one lab he was lucky enough to record a major new breakthrough as it actually occurred. A post-doctoral researcher was presenting a finding to the group that he could not explain. He knew from work with rabbits that there are distinct cells associated with a disease of the joints and a disease of the heart, but looking at a human subject he had found both these types of cells together in the heart. Both the joints and the heart are areas strongly shielded by the immune system. The lab director was interested and asked why the researcher thought that both cells could penetrate the immune system in the heart. He did not know. The director focused the question down to what the two cells could have in common to enable them to pass the immune system defences of the heart. Now the researcher made an analogy to another experiment in the lab which had found that a common property of two different cells enabled them to access an area.[xi] Suddenly the whole lab had a spark of collective insight realizing that the property that enabled the cells to penetrate the immune system was not connected to the property that caused the disease. In the following informal brainstorming sessions lots of analogies were made between the immune system in rabbits and that in humans and suggestions were made for further experiments. The group had started the meeting thinking that there were two distinct disease cells, a disease cell specialized for joints and one specialized for the heart, they now realized that they had found a common property of cells unconnected to these diseases that enabled them to pass through the human immune system. This conceptual shift had powerful implications for understanding human auto-immune diseases and led to new products and new prizes for the lab.

Some groups are more creative than others. So what kind of group processes support creativity and what kind hinder it? Kevin Dunbar did not only study the lab referred to above, he also recorded the talk in three other microbiology laboratories over the same period of time. He found that analogies of the kind that had proved so important to the breakthrough described above were common in three of the labs and were connected to insights and to new discoveries. However, there was one lab with top-rank scientists which made no new discoveries. In this lab Dunbar found that no analogies were used. Digging a little deeper, the reason for this turned out to be that all the researchers shared the same specialized background and had developed a shared precise technical language for communication such that analogies were simply not needed. The need to explain yourself to others who do not immediately share your own way of seeing things leads to the production of analogies and metaphors which may themselves, in turn, lead others and yourself to see the object under discussion in a new way. In short, some ambiguity in meanings, misunderstanding and difference between perspectives seem to be good for creativity in conversations.

An easy way for the non-creative lab in Dunbar's study to become more creative would be to introduce non-specialists or specialists in different areas into their conversations. The presence of a non-specialist in combination with social ground rules which supported free and open communication would lead to the production of more metaphors and analogies and new ways of seeing the problems which in turn might lead to more breakthroughs. A classic example of how an analogy from outside the field of study helped a scientific advance is Friedrich Kekulé's claim to have discovered the ring-like structure of benzene after dreaming of a serpent biting its own tail. A serpent biting its own tail is a common symbol in alchemy called the 'Ouroboros' so perhaps if Kekulé had included an alchemist in his lab team and done some more brainstorming he would have made this discovery sooner. However, Dunbar warns us against the overemphasis on the role of what he calls 'distant analogies' for scientific breakthroughs. The analogies he saw being useful were often very specific and drawn from detailed knowledge of the field under investigation. It seems that creativity is no substitute for doing one's homework and knowing one's field really well. On the other hand, rich and detailed content knowledge alone without any spark of creativity will not lead to any new discoveries. It may be that often the creative spark is not a big inspiration like Kekulé's dream of a dancing snake biting its own tail but a combination of lots of little sparks in conversations, but the need for a creative spark of some sort is real enough. The source of creative sparks is probably not to be found in the spiritual realm or in the unconscious mind but lies in the dialogic gap which we introduced in Chapter 2. Communicating across this gap between people with different experiences and different perspectives inevitably leads to new ways of thinking and seeing expressed in new metaphors and analogies.

Creative talk in business: The horse's arse

The example of a scientific breakthrough described above relied on local analogies shared between specialists with slightly different experience. However, Keith Sawyer provides us with a marvellous example of how any experience whatsoever can prove to be a rich resource in creative conversations. The example is taken originally from the literature on 'synectics', a technique widely used to foster creativity in business contexts.[xii] The technique is to use brainstorming but to build on this with activities designed to promote and develop new analogies. One synectics group was asked to design a dispenser for sticky liquids like nail polish or glue that did not need a stopper or lid. The challenge was to keep the liquid sealed off from the air to avoid it going hard and keeping the dispenser opening from gumming up. Using the synectics approach which encourages seeking analogies the group tried various ways of approaching the problem, like the way clams come out of their shells and the way the human mouth works in spitting out bits of chewed up food, but none of them worked. Then one member of the group recalled his childhood on an old-fashioned farm where he had often sat behind dray horses on a hay cart:

> 'When a horse would take a crap, first his outer . . . I guess you could call it a mouth, would open. Then the anal sphincter would dilate and a horse ball would come out. Afterwards everything would close up again. The whole picture would be clean as a whistle.'

The others questioned him closely about how the horse dealt with diarrhoea and so on and then designed and built a dispenser to operate just like a horse's arse. I like this story because it illustrates that, since everyone has a different range of experiences, there is no telling where the next useful insight will come from. While insight might leap from the findings of a big government funded research study it might equally emerge from a horse's arse.

Creative talk in practice

The main implications for education of the research I report in this chapter seem to be threefold:

1   that playful talk and improvisation games in which people respond to each other with odd associations and new strange ways of seeing things are the baseline of creative thought and should be valued in classrooms as well as elsewhere.
2   educational tasks and activities should be designed so that they build on and channel imagination and playful talk rather than, as so often happens, dismissing such talk as 'off-task'.
3   one way to help fashion spontaneous creative play into more valued products, both new products and new educational understandings, is through the kind of open-ended questions and sequences of questions that lead children to reflect on the connections and patterns in their experience.

Teaching talk in classrooms is clearly valuable but the Exploratory Talk programme described in the previous chapter is more geared towards explicit reasoning than towards creativity. In studies of Exploratory Talk around reasoning test problems referred to in the previous chapter, Chapter 2, children frequently rejected the suggestions of others saying something like: 'No, I don't agree because of x, y, z'. They were taught to use language in this way. But in the examples of creative talk given above such explicit challenges can be inappropriate: for example, it would be unlikely that anyone would reply to Alex's claim that you can see the radiator as a big bone by saying 'No, I don't agree, because...'. Creative play with words and ideas assumes an orientation of mutual trust and support where each participant knows that what he or she says will be accepted. Instead of challenging, the participants try to make the best sense they can of a different perspective, and this effort to listen and understand opens up a space of reflection in which ideas can resonate together and new ideas can emerge.

The spirit of dialogic creative talk is well represented by Anna Craft's suggestion that teaching for creativity be conceptualized in terms of encouraging 'possibility thinking', an idea which includes fashioning new products as well as coming up with new ideas and finding new problems as well as solving encountered problems.[xiii] Possibility thinking, she argues, is exemplified through the posing, in multiple ways, of the question 'What if?'. This relates to Guy Claxton's suggestion that instead of teaching things as if they were simply true teachers should always raise the possibility that things could be different by saying 'might be' in place of 'is'.[xiv] In practice, aspects of teaching for possibility thinking in classrooms include:

- Posing questions
- Play
- Immersion and making connections
- Being imaginative
- Innovation
- Risk taking
- Self determination[xv]

The effectiveness of this approach has been evaluated in a number of studies in primary classrooms using interviews and ethnographic observation.[xvi] These evaluations suggest that teaching can promote more of what I have called creativity 1, or simply coming up with a new idea, and also more creativity 2, fashioning of socially valued products. In this context socially valued products are the sort of artworks, ideas and essays that are desired within the school curriculum.

The key for moving from creativity 1 to creativity 2 seems to be the reflective and stimulating nature of the questions asked by teachers and others. There are many activities designed to promote and improve the creative quality of questions. One activity taken from the Head Start programme in the USA seems to exemplify these:

1   Pick an everyday object or topic and brainstorm a list of questions about it.
2   Look over the list and transform some of the questions into questions that challenge the imagination. Do this by transforming questions along the lines of:
    - What would it be like if . . . ?
    - How would it be different if . . . ?
    - Suppose that . . . ?
    - What change if . . . ?
    - How would it look differently if . . . ?
3   Choose a question to explore imaginatively. Explore it by imaginatively playing out its possibilities. Do this by: writing a story or essay, drawing a picture, creating a play or dialogue, inventing a scenario, conducting an imaginary interview, conducting a thought experiment.
4   Reflect: What new ideas do you have about the topic, concept or object that you didn't have before?[xvii]

Some open questions that encourage creative thinking in the context of science lessons could be:

What do you notice about . . . ?
What can you tell me about . . . ?
What does it remind you of?
Which things do you think belong together? Why do you think that?
What do you think will happen next?

What happened after you did that?
Why do you think that happened? I wonder why it did that?
Do you think you could do it differently?
I wonder what made you think that?
Anything else? Or?[xviii]

The most valuable type of question for developing creativity is often referred to as the 'What if...?' question. 'What ifs' can be applied to every area of the curriculum.

> **Literacy:** *If* we make the good characters evil and the evil characters good then how would the plot of the story be affected?
>
> **History:** *If* you were time transported from a present-day town to a Tudor town what differences would you see?
>
> **Science:** *If* we add ink to the water then what do you think will happen to the flower?[xix]

Questions for stimulating creative ideas about any topic can be grouped under the mnemonic **CREATE**:

> **C**ombine: Can you add something else to it? Can you combine purposes, ideas?
>
> **R**earrange: Can parts of it be moved or changed?
>
> **E**liminate: What could you remove or replace – in part or whole? Can it be simplified?
>
> **A**dapt: Can it be adapted? What else is this like? What ideas does it suggest?
>
> **T**ry another use: Can it be put to other uses – or given a new use if you changed one part?
>
> **E**xtend: What could be added – words, pictures, symbols, functions, decoration, logos?[xx]

I referred to the technique of synectics that goes beyond brainstorming to encourage people to create links between thoughts and images that had not previously been connected. One of the techniques used in synectics is the 'excursion', simply the process of taking a mental break from the problem, generating seemingly irrelevant material and connecting it to a problem or task, to create a new way of thinking about it. This may include drawing, storytelling, taking a walk, making collages, generating metaphors, analogies, paradoxes or anything the facilitator decides to introduce. It is interesting to note that in one project which tried to implement synectics in primary classrooms, the team purposefully did not provide teachers with a list of readymade applications, but aimed to empower them to invent their own applications. The idea here is that this approach to continuing professional development is likely to promote more sustainable and transferable skills.

One excursion invented by a teacher on this project for her Year 1 (5 and 6-year-old) children was a 'connections game'. The children had played the game before and enjoyed it as it involves a lot of activity and excitement. Sally reminded them of the rules by acting them out and modelling the creative behaviours herself. They were talking about Guy Fawkes in a circle when she introduced the excursion activity saying:

'I'm going to walk round the circle and we need to make the circle quite small, 'cos I'm going to walk round. I'm going to keep thinking of something connected with "Parliament". So we go round . . . ' [Walks round, touching children on head saying "Parliament". When she reaches Josh, she says] ' "King". Now Josh is going to try and catch me.' [Runs around circle trying to beat Josh back to his space in the circle.] 'Josh, would you like to start at Joseph with "King". When you think of something that connects with "King" then you need to try and steal their place.'

During the course of this game the chain of connections made by the children was 'king' → 'government' → 'queen' → 'princess' → 'prince' and, finally, back to 'government' at which point the game ended. For young children sitting still and discussing for long periods is quite difficult and these 'excursion' activities help to shake things up and get more creative and playful talk flowing.[xxi]

Conclusion

The focus on classroom talk, which I described in the previous chapter about dialogic education, has tended to overlook creativity in favour of explicit reasoning. However, on closer inspection, even the relatively hard thinking involved in solving standard reasoning tests depends upon creativity. Contrary to the popular myth of the lone genius, research suggests that most useful creativity stems from new ideas and analogies that emerge within dialogues. The everyday talk of children is already creative in that it is full of imaginative leaps and almost random links. However, the concept of creativity has two poles, imaginative play (creativity 1) and the fashioning of socially valued products (creativity 2). Children's playful talk is not very productive or useful but it should be valued as a rich resource for more educationally constructive dialogues. Moving from creativity 1, just playing around, to creativity 2, creating something of value, can be achieved in the classroom through the use of ground rules for talk and focused reflective questions. These ground rules and activities need to both encourage 'What if?' thinking and also question new analogies in order to select and shape them towards new product designs (like a new word for a newsletter) and new insights (like understanding a reasoning test problem). Understanding something truly new is a creative act for the child, building links between ideas and areas of experience that were previously separate. Stimulating and directing playful talk is one way to promote more spontaneous creative understanding within the curriculum.

Chapter Summary

In the past most studies of creativity have focused on individuals but in this chapter I described creativity as a property of classroom talk. I introduced that 'playful talk' which is a baseline for much children's talk and I showed how it represents a resource for thinking. I described several examples where careful reflective questioning harnessed the creativity of playful talk and directed it towards the solution of problems. The same creative process was at work, I argued, in English where two girls constructed a newsletter together, in philosophy where a group of children learnt to think about and understand aspects of their lives, and also in mathematics and science where underlying structures were revealed by the use of new metaphors and analogies. I ended with examples of how playful talk can be supported in classrooms and directed, through questioning, towards understanding within the curriculum.

4 Creative understanding

Chapter Overview

In this chapter I get quite theoretical and try to take you through an argument for why I think that creativity is rooted in dialogic relations and what I call 'dialogic space', the infinite space of potentiality that opens up within the gap between voices in dialogue. In the previous chapter I introduced the creativity that is present in playful talk and how this can be shaped to provide new insights and understandings. In this chapter I argue that if creativity comes from 'dialogic' relations then so does understanding a new idea in the classroom. The chapter ends with some ideas and tips for promoting the capacity to be more creative in the classroom, which is also, I argue, a way to teach for more understanding.

Understanding understanding

The new primary curriculum in the UK stresses the importance of teaching for understanding but what is *understanding* exactly? Sometimes understanding just means fitting new things into familiar frameworks. So if a 10-year-old comes across the phrase 'Buddy can you spare a dime' and asks 'What's a dime?' you can explain that it is a small unit of money, like a 5p bit or a 10p bit (10 cents actually) and they will probably understand. But they only understand because they already know what money is and they can fit this new fact into that existing knowledge. But then how do you explain 'dime' to a very young child who does not know what money is? Money is mysterious stuff. Children's questions can help us to see again just how strange and wonderful it is that a silver coin can be exchanged for a chocolate bar in a shop. This kind of understanding, understanding that involves something really new, is often referred to as conceptual change.

According to Micheline ('Micki') Chi, author of the 'categorical shift' theory of conceptual change, children are often held back in the classroom because they insist on understanding new things in old ways. For example, some children never shift from understanding 'force' as the sort of influence that gets exerted in playground disputes as in 'It's not my fault, he forced me to do it'. They think of force as the 'forcefulness' of people and objects and do not shift to understand force as an abstract property of interactions. The children who do not shift remain baffled; how could the kind of force that kids exert in the playground act at a distance in the form of gravity to cause an apple to fall onto Newton's head?

Micki Chi begins one of her articles on conceptual change with the claim that 'The essence of creativity is to see a situation or an object from two frames of reference or two unrelated "matrices of thought"'.[i] She argues that conceptual change in the classroom is essentially creative. It requires a re-representation from one way of seeing things to another new way of seeing things. Because lots of connections are then made all at once and everything 'falls into place' this is experienced as an 'Aha' moment. Understanding in this 'categorical shift' sense is a creative event for the child concerned, even if they are learning something that has been learnt a million times before by others. Therefore to understand understanding in the classroom we need first to understand creativity. Explaining creativity might help us plan for teaching that will lead to conceptual change and so to deeper understanding. But even if it does not help us in the classroom, trying to understand creativity is always a fascinating struggle.

Rescuing the idea of creativity as a thinking skill

In the last chapter I argued that the analysis of classroom talk supports Keith Sawyer's claim that creativity does not usually take the form of a fully formed inspiration granted to a single creative person. Creativity more normally occurs in dialogues and takes the form of lots of little sparks of insight that add up to a significant new view of the world or perhaps contribute to the creation of a new product. This rethinking of creativity as something that is collective and that often occurs through dialogues in groups is an important contribution to the debate about creativity. However, it does not mean that the mystery of the origin of creativity has been completely dissolved. If creativity occurs in lots of little sparks in dialogues and thoughts then we still have to ask, where do those little sparks of insight and originality come from?

I think that creativity is one fruit of the dialogic relation which I described in Chapter 2. Creativity, in however small and everyday a form, always seems to involve a leap from one way of seeing things to another. This is certainly the case with the kind of conceptual change that requires a shift in the way in which we understand ideas in the classroom. I argue that the gap that is crossed over in any creative leap of this kind is always a version of the dialogic gap I introduced in Chapter 2. This was described as the gap between different perspectives or ways of seeing that are held in tension together. The dialogic gap is not just an ordinary boundary between two separate things as if seen from the outside. The dialogic boundary is inclusive and dynamic. When experienced from the inside the transition from one perspective to another means crossing a kind of no-man's-land that belongs to neither side but is pregnant with new possibilities.

A number of people now argue that we do not need a notion of creativity as a separate thinking skill. They argue that what we often describe as creativity can be explained away by more prosaic notions like ambition, luck and hard work. In his fascinating book *Outliers: The story of success* Malcolm Gladwell[ii] seems to make this claim, pointing out that successes in any field all turn out to have practised their craft for at least 10,000 hours. Even Mozart, apparently, was only hailed as an infant prodigy because he started practising music very young and so he was able to get in his 10,000 hours early.

Hard work is often important to success, of course, but this does not mean that we can do without a notion of creativity. We can easily see why this is so in classrooms. Children who work equally hard at mathematics or history or whatever subject will understand the underlying concepts at a very different rate. Some leap up to new levels of conceptual understanding quickly while others just cannot seem to get new ways of seeing things however many times you present these to them in however many different ways. In the research I described in Chapter 2, we found that some children can see the underlying patterns behind reasoning test puzzles quickly and others cannot. Creative thinking, as Guy Claxton puts it, is simply the skill of coming up with a new idea when you need one. This is what makes the difference between being 'quick' or being 'slow' at grasping new ideas. My argument is that this skill is not rooted in genetic differences, although of course genes may play a part, but is essentially a dialogic skill. Just as we found that we could teach children how to see the patterns more easily in reasoning test puzzles so we can teach children how to be more creative.

According to one popular 'socio-cultural' account, teaching is all about helping children learn to use cultural tools.[iii] Cultural tools include words and concepts and even stories. This is a very useful account of lots of different kinds of learning but I have not found it useful to explain learning to be more creative because it is not clear where the 'cultural tool' of creativity is or what it would look like.

To explore further the roots of creativity I will begin by going back to re-examine the original 'Eureka' moment that became a legendary illustration of creativity. I jokingly refer to this as a search for the 'Eureka' tool but of course I do not think that the skill of creativity is a cultural tool. I hope to persuade you that the source of the 'Eureka' moment lies in the essentially inside-outside/outside-in way in which we think that comes from dialogues. However, I have said far too much already; let me tell you a story that I hope will show you more clearly what I mean.

The 'Eureka' tool?

'Aha' moments, when understanding dawns for the first time, are also commonly referred to as 'Eureka' moments. This refers back to perhaps the most famous recorded creative breakthrough when Archimedes first understood how to solve a problem that he had been struggling with and was so overcome with excitement that he leapt out of his bath shouting 'Eureka!' (ancient Greek for 'I have found it'). Reportedly, he then rushed naked into the street forgetting even to get dressed in his enthusiasm to try out his new idea. I am going to reconstruct this first Eureka event in the hope that something in its form might give us an insight into the nature of Eureka moments in general.

Archimedes lived in the Greek city state of Syracuse nearly two thousand three hundred years ago. He used to do small jobs for the then king of Syracuse, King Hiero II. The king had ordered a new gold crown and he had given the goldsmiths enough gold to make it. The crown he had been given back weighed the same as the gold that he had given out but nonetheless he was suspicious. He thought that the goldsmiths might have diluted the gold with a cheaper base metal in order to sell some of the gold on for their own profit. He asked Archimedes to play the detective and find out for him. Of course Archimedes was not allowed to damage the crown, so he could not melt it down into a regularly shaped body in order to calculate its density. After struggling with the problem for a while the solution came to him unexpectedly. While getting into his bath he noticed that the level of the water in the tub rose as he got in. He suddenly realized that this effect could be used to determine the volume of the crown. The submerged crown would displace an amount of water equal to its own volume. By dividing the weight of the crown by the volume of water displaced, the density of the crown could be ascertained. This density would be lower than that of gold if cheaper less dense metals had been added. It was at that very moment that Archimedes took to the streets naked crying 'Eureka!'.

Let us break this problem down a little to see how it was solved. First, we have the crown:

Figure 4.1 Crown

Archimedes probably looked at this and studied it and tried to break it down into its constituent geometric shapes so that he could work out the density, but a way to do this eluded him. The real crown was reportedly shaped like a laurel wreath so it was impossible to break that down into units that could be measured.

In his workshop Archimedes had various tools for solving problems, like measures and weighing scales but, like all cultural tools, these could only help him solve problems of a kind that he had solved before. None of his available tools could help him solve this problem, because it was new to him. This is the essential problem with cultural tools, they only help you solve problems that are already known about. Those who argue that thinking is some sort of cultural tool use have to ask themselves: what is the 'Eureka' tool that Archimedes needed at this point?

The source of Archimedes' 'Eureka' insight was to focus not on the object but on the background to the object, the water displaced by the object.

Figure 4.2   Crown seen as a space left behind in water

In this case the 'Eureka' tool was a shift in perspective from foreground to background or from representing the crown as an object to representing it as a space displacing water (see Figure 4.2). A more generalized version of the same tool is re-representing things to see them from different perspectives or points of view.

I am referring to Archimedes' ability to re-represent his problem in order to see it from a new and unexpected perspective as the 'Eureka' tool as a joke in order to tease those who claim that all our thinking is mediated by cultural tools. Archimedes had a workshop full of tools and a library stocked with all the mathematical and scientific procedures of his day: he needed his 'Eureka' experience precisely because no existing cultural tool would do the job for him. After this experience he is said to have built a new tool to help his apprentices find out if base metal had been mixed with gold. Cultural tools always embody previous solutions in this way. The 'Eureka' experience itself is never a cultural tool because it is always new and unique.

And yet this does not mean that the 'Eureka' experience has no indirect source within a culture. It is extraordinary how much invention and creative thought came out of the ancient Greek world at the time of Archimedes. It may not be a coincidence that ancient Greek culture encouraged public dialogue and was the source of democracy as a method of government. Although Archimedes served a king when he had his 'Eureka' moment, his home city of Syracuse had been a democracy before this particular king's reign and it was at the heart of many trade routes with much interchange of ideas as well as of goods.

We do not need to travel to ancient Greece to see 'Eureka' moments, we can see them dawn on young children's faces in primary classrooms every day. I describe a classic 'Eureka' moment in the next chapter, Chapter 5, when the light of understanding arrives very visibly for Angelina who has been resisting an argument about how to make graphs. Then, with the help of some imaginary perspective-taking, she finally gets the point and says 'Ohhh' very slowly while raising her gaze upwards and opening her eyes wider and wider: 'Ohhh . . . I see it now', she repeats slowly as if with a sense of wonder.

I argued in Chapter 2 that our first experience of taking a new perspective on things comes when we learn to see not only with our own infant eyes but also as if with the eyes of our mother, following her gaze to see what she is pointing at. It is only once we have achieved that ability to re-represent the world as if from the point of view of another person that we are able to engage in play, giving words and ideas to our toys as if they had their own point of view on the world too. Even solitary thinkers like Archimedes in his bath can think in a way that is highly 'dialogic' in that it consists in leaps between perspectives. This ability to leap between perspectives is something that he must have first learnt in dialogues with others and then internalized to be able to continue the dialogues even when alone.

Chiasm and creativity

If we know that personal creativity begins in the context of real dialogues, like the dialogues between a parent and a child, and that it always exhibits the dialogic structure of a reversal of perspectives, this is a start towards an explanation of creativity. However, it is only a start. The question that then occurs is, why should this dialogic structure of a reversal between perspectives lead to creativity? Creativity, after all, is about new perspectives, not about a dialogue between existing perspectives. Maurice Merleau-Ponty, a French philosopher, who was for a long time good friends with Jean-Paul Sartre, sheds some light on this question. He is less well known than Sartre, probably, some say, because he was the better philosopher; less prone to grand public gestures and more concerned with the careful analysis of experience.

Maurice Merleau-Ponty describes how the painter Matisse was once filmed at work on a canvas and then the film was played back to him in slow motion. The effect was extraordinary. Matisse, seen with the naked eye, worked without hesitation moving confidently from stroke to stroke. The slow motion playback, however, showed that before each stroke the brush hovered and danced in front of the canvas, as if many different possibilities were being tried out until at last the brush descended to make a single mark. Even in the process of each brush stroke Matisse was, quite unconsciously, exploring a space of possibilities before finally, as Merleau-Ponty puts it, he 'brought his brush toward the line which called for it in order that the painting might finally be that which it was in the process of becoming'.[iv] This suggests that between the seeing and the creating of a scene there seems to be a space of possibilities that Matisse's brush inhabits, a perceptual version of dialogic space perhaps?

Merleau-Ponty analyses this creativity in terms of a kind of dialogue between the painter here and now making marks on the canvas and the emerging vision of the final future work. His reference to the artist, in a sense, facilitating the emergence of a final painting, rather than just imposing ideas on a canvas, brings to mind a famous quotation attributed to Michelangelo. When he was asked how he managed to carve such a lifelike appearance out of a block of marble he replied: 'I saw the angel in the marble and carved until I set him free'. Of course I am not trying to claim here that there were real angels in the marble and that only Michelangelo was sensitive enough see them. My claim is only that creative people (that means all of us, of course! – examine your own experience of creativity to tell me if this is right or wrong) often do not feel that they are in conscious control of the creative process. They often claim to feel called to express something that wants to be expressed but that seems to come to them from outside. Part of creativity is learning to surrender conscious control in order to allow voices that want to speak to speak through you.

Merleau-Ponty uses the word 'chiasm' to characterize his theory of perception which is also a theory of creativity and a theory of thinking. In rhetoric the term chiasm refers to the reversal of subject and object in a sentence. Reversing the sentence 'I see the world' into the sentence 'The world sees me' leads to an example of a chiasm: 'I see the world, the world sees me'.

In creativity, according to Merleau-Ponty, it is as if there are always two 'voices' like this in dialogue together, an inside voice and an outside voice. One voice is Matisse making marks on the canvas and the other voice is the future art work calling to Matisse telling him where to put the marks to bring the future painting into being. One voice is Michelangelo chipping away at a block of marble with a hammer and the other voice is the angel trapped inside the marble calling to be released. One voice is our own voice as we struggle to express ourselves in jumbled up words that are never quite right and the other voice is the quiet but insistent voice of the idea that wants to be expressed.

Figure 4.3   Chiasm

Merleau-Ponty's chiasm idea can be summed up by the illustration in Figure 4.3. Chiasm is the idea that you can either see the figure (the candlestick) or you can see the ground (the two faces) but you cannot properly see both at once. However, both sides, figure and ground, depend upon each other and can reverse around each other. I think that Merleau Ponty's understanding that perception is chiasmic, art is chiasmic and dialogue is chiasmic, can help us to understand the source of creativity. But before I try to turn Merleau-Ponty's chiasm concept into a useful theory of creativity for primary education I want to look briefly at some other insights into creativity coming from the discipline of psychology.

Flow: A view of creativity from psychology

Mihalyi Csíkszentmihályi (pronounced chick-sent-me-high-ee) is probably the leading contemporary psychologist of creativity. He is most famous for the concept of 'flow' in creativity; people enter a 'flow state' when they are fully absorbed in activity during which they lose their sense of time and have feelings of great satisfaction. Csíkszentmihályi describes 'flow' as:

> being completely involved in an activity for its own sake. The ego falls away. Time flies. Every action, movement, and thought follows inevitably from the previous one, like playing jazz. Your whole being is involved, and you're using your skills to the utmost.[v]

The concept of 'flow' came out of a major research study.[vi] Csíkszentmihályi and his team interviewed 91 people who could be called creative because they had transformed their field in a publicly acknowledged way, scientists who had won the Nobel Prize, artists who were leaders of new movements and so on. He found that when they really engaged with their field and with producing new ideas or products, all reported a sense of joy and of inner reward. Some reported that the quality of time itself changed from being the external context of actions to becoming an internal flow in which awareness of the passage of time disappeared. So many creative people described being carried along by a current that Csíkszentmihályi decided upon the word 'flow' to describe this state. *Flow* is the mental state of operation in which the person is fully immersed in what he or she is doing, characterized by a feeling of energized focus, full involvement, and success in the process of the activity. A key component is the loss of a division between self and world.

Csíkszentmihályi identifies the following features as often but not always accompanying an experience of 'flow':

1   *Clear goals* (expectations and rules are discernible and goals are attainable and align appropriately with one's skill set and abilities).
2   *Concentrating and focusing*, a high degree of concentration on a limited field of attention (a person engaged in the activity will have the opportunity to focus and to delve deeply into it).
3   *A loss of the feeling of self-consciousness*, the merging of action and awareness.

4   *Distorted sense of time*, one's subjective experience of time is altered.
5   Direct and immediate *feedback* (successes and failures in the course of the activity are apparent, so that behaviour can be adjusted as needed).
6   *Balance between ability level and challenge* (the activity is neither too easy nor too difficult).
7   A sense of personal *control* over the situation or activity.
8   The activity is *intrinsically rewarding*, so there is an effortlessness of action.
9   People become absorbed in their activity, and the focus of awareness is narrowed down to the activity itself, *action awareness merging*.[vii]

Csíkszentmihályi's research focused on individual creativity rather than on creative dialogues and creative group work but it did not ignore conversations. According to Keith Sawyer, who was one of Csíkszentmihályi's research students at Chicago University: '*Csíkszentmihályi found that the most common place people experienced flow was in conversation with others*'.[viii]

While 'flow' is a very valuable description of what creativity feels like from within, it is not really a theory of creativity. Csíkszentmihályi offers a socio-cultural systems model through which creativity is to be found in the interaction of the individual with his or her 'field' which includes all the 'gatekeepers' who select what new work will be recognized or not and the 'domain' which is the part of culture in which the individual and the field are located such as maths, physics or fine art. For something to be called Creativity with a capital 'C' he writes that the creative individual's work has to be recognized by his or her field as transforming the domain in some way.

The system model of creativity advocated by Csíkszentmihályi is useful in drawing our attention to how social processes can encourage or hinder creativity. It points out that creativity is not just an individual thing but is also a social thing and it gives us some pointers on how to make a community more creative. For instance, a school could become more creative if there is a better mechanism for recognizing and disseminating good new ideas. Why not have an ideas box for children in the school to put in ideas and publicly reward the person who comes up with the best idea?

However, a description of how a society recognizes creativity is not the same at all as explaining the real lived phenomenon of creativity in the act. While a socio-cultural systems model of the kind Csíkszentmihályi advances might answer the question 'How does something get to be called "Creativity"?' that is not quite the same as the question I would like to ask, which is, 'What is creativity really?'.[ix]

The evidence that Csíkszentmihályi collected from creative people suggests that, whatever the social recognition, creativity is something very real for these people leading, for example, to a different experience of time. If creativity leads to a different experience of time then I want to know why. Here, I think that an explanation of real creativity can be found by combining the more descriptive studies of psychologists like Csíkszentmihályi and his former student Sawyer with the insights and theories of philosophers like Merleau-Ponty.

Creativity as essentially dialogic

Freeman Dyson, who made a major contribution to quantum theory, was interviewed by Csíkszentmihályi in his big study of creativity. Like many creative people he echoed the point made first by Michelangelo, that creative work seems to have two sides to it. He describes how, after he immersed himself intensively in reading the relevant literature about a cutting edge problem in physics, he took a break and went touring across California. The solution to the problem suddenly came to him and he felt impelled to write it down. He writes of his experience of creativity:

> I always find that when I am writing, it is really the fingers that are doing it and not the brain. Somehow the writing takes charge. And the same thing happens of course with equations.... The trick is to start from both ends and to meet in the middle, which is essentially like building a bridge.[x]

Summing up the findings of his interviews with creative people Csíkszentmihályi adds:

> Creative thoughts evolve in this gap filled with tension – holding on to what is known and accepted while tending towards a still ill-defined truth that is barely glimpsed on the other side of the chasm. Even when thoughts incubate below the threshold of consciousness, this tension is present.[xi]

Csíkszentmihályi's interviewees describe losing their sense of a separate self and losing their sense of being contained within normal clock time. Merleau-Ponty's chiasm coupled with the dialogic theory I introduced in Chapter 2 can explain exactly what is happening in the flow of engaged creativity.

Dialogic theory is not just about dialogue. The dialogic principle is that two or more perspectives held together in the tension of relationship open a space of potential new meaning. At the heart of our world we find not fixed things – not identity – but a kind of relationship or non-identity. The gap between me and you in a dialogue is not just a physical gap. It is 'constitutive' which means that it is only because of the gap between us that I can know me and that you can know you. In other words the dialogic gap is not part of the world: it is an opening onto the continuous act of the creation of the world. Creativity is possible because, instead of identifying with the fixed identities that we construct on either side of the gap, we learn to return to the gap and identify with the space of the gap. Instead of a fixed 'me' on one side and a fixed 'you' on the other, in a real dialogue we can enter into the space between us and learn to see ourselves anew from there.

Merleau-Ponty's studies of perception and of visual art suggest that the same dialogic pattern applies to creativity in general. It is not only true that I touch the world, the world also touches me. According to Merleau-Ponty my physical image of myself and my physical image of the world is constructed out of this intertwined 'sensing and being sensed' process. When I say that our perceptual world is constructed in this way I mean the world of space and time that we inhabit. Merleau-Ponty's chiasm idea is the claim that the gap between me and the world, or between the sentient and the sensed as he puts it, is not really a physical gap, but a kind of hinge around which the perspectives of outside and inside turn around each other. This hinge or gap (écart) between the inside perspective and the outside perspective is an opening on the unknowable outside of experience. Out of this opening of potential we construct images of the world on that side and the body on this side but really we are always on both sides at once. In creative thinking we inhabit this gap between opposites which is always there before the solidification of forms. To teach for creativity is therefore to encourage a shift in identification back from fixed forms towards the original opening or gap that gives all forms birth. To put this another way, Merleau-Ponty's hinge or gap opens up into the space of possibilities in which the creative artist can re-imagine the world differently.

A visual presentation of the main argument

Some readers might find what I am trying to say here a bit obscure. The dialogic gap I introduced in Chapter 2 and Merleau-Ponty's chiasm represent a way of thinking about difference that is relatively new and many people find it challenging. Normally we think in terms of identity and assume an already constructed world in which differences are negatively defined as the difference between existing things. The rethinking of the significance of difference that I rely on in my argument about creativity is sometimes associated with post-modernism. It was begun by Heidegger[xii] and taken up in different ways by Merleau-Ponty[xiii] and also by Jacques Derrida.[xiv] Essentially this rethinking offers a more positive account of difference as being a creative force at the origin of every type of identity.

Derrida seems to claim that this argument is impossible to understand because the way we understand things is inevitably structured in terms of identity. But I want to prove him wrong. I think that the shift from identity thinking to difference thinking is easy to understand. To make this proof I need your help. I have developed a simple visual argument that I think makes the case for difference thinking quite clear. Does it work?

Step 1: Think of a thing, anything

Ordinarily we think we inhabit a world of things with clear identities demarcated by boundaries. This is the way that thought works. Think of a thing, anything at all, and you will be able to draw some sort of boundary around it in your mind. Even if your 'thing' is something vague like 'happiness' it is still separated by a boundary from other feelings like 'sadness' or 'fear'. As discussed above, the way in which we draw a boundary around 'now' to separate it from 'then' and a boundary around 'here' to separate it from 'there' and a boundary around 'self' to separate it from 'other' all follow this same general pattern. This is illustrated by Figure 4.4: Identity.

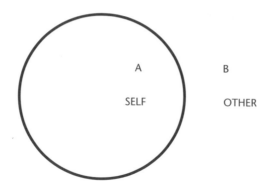

Figure 4.4 Identity

A boundary around a space illustrates this basic building block of thinking: a thing with an identity. Classical logic begins with the idea of identity that 'a thing is what it is and not another thing', a claim written formally as A = A and A ≠ B.[xv] But identity is also used to refer to people, contrasting me as 'self' to you as 'other'. This seems like common sense. It should do because it is the basic structure of consciousness. Experiencing a figure on a ground is simply what it means to be conscious. However, there is more to reality that our conscious experience of it.

Step 2: But what must have happened already to make this picture possible?

Figure 4.4: Identity, presupposes that someone somehow has already drawn a line separating the figure (A) from the background (B). This act of drawing a line around a thing is 'constitutive' because it brings the thing into existence in the first place (see Figure 4.5). Since we need the figure-ground structure to be self conscious we cannot be

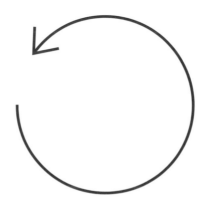

Figure 4.5 Drawing a boundary line

conscious of the prior movement constituting a figure-ground relationship by drawing a difference, but we can work backwards from experience to figure out that this must have happened in order for us to be conscious. To put this another way, since I only come into existence as me after I have separated a 'me' from a 'you' (and a 'now' from a 'then' etc.) I could not possibly be conscious of this prior movement of creation of my world.

And, of course, drawing a boundary to create an identity (Figure 4.5) presupposes a field that one draws the boundary within. In this case, the underlying sheet of paper upon which one draws.

Figure 4.6 The background sheet of paper

A figure always appears against a ground but in looking at the figure we often ignore the ground. Figure 4.6, a sheet of paper, is just symbolic of the kind of background space which must be assumed if we are to make a constitutive difference by drawing a boundary around a figure.

Every figure is a figure standing out against a particular background. The poet Mallarmé, for example, spoke of how the white page in front of him before he wrote upon it was already pregnant with all possible meanings.[xvi] By drawing a letter or a word on the page he brought out some of those meanings but always at the expense of other possible meanings. These are metaphors and analogies but they point to a pre-existing space of infinite possible meanings that is then carved up into particular figure-ground configurations.

So, to recap, my argument is we normally live in a world of bounded things that include 'me' and 'you'; 'self' and 'other'. This world, the world of our experience (not to be confused with the real underlying structures explored by science),[xvii] must be constructed by a movement of drawing a boundary around things. The space where this movement of drawing a boundary happens is not the physical space and time that we experience, because this is the world that we can only experience after a lot of boundaries have been drawn. This implies that there is another kind of space underlying the boundaries, a space of possibility before boundaries become fixed.

Dialogic space, the space of meaning that we enter into when we engage in dialogue together, is not a physical space, so where does it come from? Dialogue, whereby the outside enters the inside and the inside enters the outside, is a way of unpicking some of the boundaries that locate us within identities. The space that dialogues open up is the space of the boundary, that is to say, the space of infinite possibility that was there before the boundary was drawn.

The chiasm again

When you walk through the night air are you feeling the breeze on your cheeks or is it rather that the breeze is touching your cheeks? The essential idea of the chiasm is that when we touch an object we are also being touched by it.

Merleau-Ponty suggests we all try a simple experiment to understand the chiasm. Shut your eyes and try touching your right hand with your left hand in order to explore its shape. Now do the same with your right hand exploring your left hand. What you may find out is that you can either experience being the touching hand, or the hand being touched, but that it is not easy to experience being both the touching hand and the touched hand at once. When you switch from being the hand that is touching to the hand that is touched, there is a tiny gap between the two perspectives. Merleau-Ponty's point here is that really we are on both sides, we are both doing the touch and being touched, just as in a dialogue we are both the one doing the talking and the one listening, reconstructing the voice of the other person. Despite this doubleness we only tend to identify ourselves as being on one side of the chiasm. Merleau-Ponty calls the gap (*écart* in French) between the touching and the being touched a hinge (in this case it is the hinge between the person as an active touching subject on the one hand and the same person as a passive touched object, on the other). Now ask yourself: where exactly is this gap located in space and time?

I want to refer you back at this point to the group of children solving a reasoning test problem together I described at the beginning of Chapter 2. Although they started with voices outside each other they ended up operating in a shared space of meaning. We can see this shared space in signs like one person starting a sentence and another finishing it with no embarrassment, or one person's words being taken up and used by another person with no sense of 'these are my words and those are your words'. Words and ideas emerge in a dialogue and it is not always clear whose words and ideas they are. The space of the dialogue is no longer just the physical space between the children. In the course of the dialogue what was at first outside, for each one of them, the voice of the other, has become inside and what was at first only inside, their own thoughts, has become outside. A new shared dialogic space has been created. This space is an inclusive boundary in that it lies between them but it includes them all within it. I illustrated this process with two concentric circles first indicating a centre of identity in each separate child's head, then both of these expanding and moving to be centred on the space between them while including them (Figures 2.2 and 2.3).

The whole of education for creativity should be understood as moving people from identification with fixed identities towards identification with the gap between identities; the gap out of which those identities were born and in which they can be re-imagined and re-forged. I do not think that this is different from Anna Craft's account of teaching for creativity as moving learners from the fixity of 'what is' and 'what must be' to the space of possibilities opened up by 'what if' and 'what might be'. What I am trying to do here is to understand good practice in teaching for creativity by providing a more theoretical understanding of what is really going on when children learn to be more creative in this way.

Creativity as stepping in and out of time

Merleau-Ponty's analysis of perception as chiasm, whereby there are always two sides that can reverse around each other, reveals that our tendency to trap ourselves on one side of the self-other and self-world divide is an illusion. In reality, thought is always born in between self and other and in between self and world in a dynamic and creative relationship. Becoming more creative is about rediscovering this truth and identifying with the living relationship in the moment, rather than with the dead images of our-selves and of others that we have constructed in the past, or that others have constructed and we have simply inherited. It is not surprising that psychologists have found that being more creative leads to an altered relationship with time. External time, or clock time, is one of the constructions that we have built out of experience. If we identify with a limited self-image or body-image then we can experience ourselves as trapped in time like a beetle in a box. But if we identify with the space of dialogue that opens out of the gap between inside and outside then we can move towards a timeless present. Perhaps, as Derrida says, we can never really experience timelessness in this sense, because ex-perience depends upon making differences. However, the descriptions of flow suggest experiences of time distortion approaching the impossible experience of a timeless now.

Think of the space of possibilities navigated by the brush of Matisse filmed in slow motion dancing just in front of the canvas. If Matisse identified not with his body or his life story but with his dancing brush then in what time would he be? The poet T.S Eliot perhaps offers the answer in a well known line: 'at the still point, there the dance is'. The poem continues: 'Except for the point, the still point, There would be no dance, and there is only the dance'.[xviii] I heard a more prosaic way of approaching this phenomenon of creative near timelessness expressed on the radio recently by the artist David Hockney, now in his seventies. Asked if life was dull for him living in Yorkshire after his swinging time in Los Angeles in the 1960s, he replied: 'Oh I never get bored me. Mind you I can get excited just looking at a puddle in Harrogate'.

99 per cent perspiration? Chiasm with a field of knowledge

I began this chapter referring to the stress on teaching for understanding found in the new primary curriculum and I claimed that teaching for understanding requires that we teach for creativity. But the curriculum also lays stress on the importance of teaching traditional knowledge areas such as science, language and mathematics. Gaining skills and knowledge in a subject area often requires hard work as well as inspiration.

In cartoons a light bulb coming on inside someone's head is often used as a symbol of the moment of creative understanding. The inventor of the light bulb, Thomas Edison, said that 'Genius is one per cent inspiration and 99 per cent perspiration'. And indeed it is often the case that understanding only comes after a lot of work doing things that you do not really understand or even enjoy.

An example often used to illustrate this claim is the need to spend long hours practising scales on a piano before being able to truly play and perhaps freely express yourself through the medium of music. I asked music educators about this and they assured me that it is really not true that learning to play an instrument needs to be boring. There are many possibilities of rewarding self-expression from the beginning. Nonetheless there is something in the idea that exciting moments of breakthrough sometimes come only after lots of less glamorous hard work. Freeman Dyson's account of his inspiration, which I quoted from briefly above, is a classic of this kind. For some months before this breakthrough he had been working very hard, reading intensively trying to solve an apparently insoluble problem in physics. The inspiration came to him suddenly only after he had relaxed and stepped back from the problem. But the new equations his fingers seemed to want to write for him were the culmination of his own hard work. It had entered inside him over a period of time from the outside, formed itself on the inside when he was not paying attention to it, and now it seemed to be welling up from the inside.

The quality of the creative expression that emerges out of the opening of dialogic space can vary considerably. When the children I quoted in the first example of the last chapter, Chapter 3: Creative Talk, engaged in playful talk they opened up a dialogic space between them but what came out were mostly TV jingles they had probably all heard the night before. I called this sort of playful talk creativity 1. But to author valuable new ideas or products, especially the sort of understandings that are valued in classrooms, these children needed to do some more homework.

The chiasm structure for creativity, whereby an inside becomes outside and an outside becomes inside, does not only apply to dialogues between two voices, it can also apply to the relationship between a person and a field of study. In learning for understanding there seems to be a chiasmic relationship stretched over time whereby the outside turns inside and then returns outside in expression.

Once I tried to learn Spanish. At first the signs and sounds of Spanish seemed outside me, they meant nothing to me. I listened to Spanish TV and I did not understand it. I forced myself to speak Spanish phrases from a book but they sounded foreign to me even as I said them. But after a period of study and lots of engaged active learning, what was at first an outside field became internalized and I found myself able to express myself in Spanish. And strangely sometimes the Spanish takes over and is expressing not the same me as when I express in English but a much more Spanish version of me with more Spanish feelings, expressions and hand movements.

The answer to the question how to teach for understanding is to teach for creativity. General creativity, the creativity that enables you to come up with a good idea when you need one, or to quickly understand the underlying patterns of a new area, consists in a facility with forming chiasmic relations. The trick is to turn everything other, everything that you don't understand, into something that you have a reversible relationship with so that, in a sense, you can be on both sides at once and see and feel from both sides at once. Of course you cannot consciously experience things from both sides at once but only from one side, however this is when you have to learn to trust the intuition that sees or feels things also from the other side. To return to the famous example of Michelangelo: it is important for children not to be left standing outside the marble block thinking about what to make, they need to be helped to listen to the voices of the angels (or whatever new voices they may hear) coming out to them from inside the marble block. OK they also need to know how to use a chisel in order to release those angels but no amount of training in chisel work will teach them how to see or hear the angels in the first place, and that is the more important skill. In their 'Aha' moments creative people get insights into what needs to be done or said in a given situation because they experience that situation from the inside as well as from the outside.

This disposition for forming chiasmic relations in every situation and at every level can be learnt through engaging in dialogues with others. Open-ended but focused questioning in dialogues can lead children to learn how to reflect on their experience in order to draw out meaning from it.

Once children have some knowledge in an area and are engaged in dialogue about it you will find that what emerges in the dialogic space that opens up is not just half digested snippets from TV jingles seen the night before but real new understandings. The chiasmic relationship remains the same for creativity 2 as for creativity 1, but for creativity 2, when this takes the form of useful understanding in the classroom, the chiasmic reversal needs to work with a mind already stocked with rich resources. To teach for creativity then it is not enough just to teach 'creativity skills' it is also necessary to teach the sort of rich content area knowledge that children can relate to, enter into and transform for themselves.

Teaching for creativity in practice

Archimedes only solved his problem when he managed to see it from a completely new and unexpected perspective. The 'Eureka tool' for thinking is simply a facility to see things in new ways. There are many educational activities and approaches that help children acquire the appropriate dispositions, habits and strategies. I mentioned a few in the last chapter and I select a few more of the best here to draw your attention to some good practice that fits the theory of creativity that I have presented.

Six hats

Edward de Bono calls the kind of thinking that Archimedes demonstrated, lateral think-ing, thinking by seeing from a new perspective, and he has devised a number of exercises to facilitate this. An approach that has been tried and tested and found to work in many schools is called the 'six thinking hats'. Each imaginary hat represents a different way of considering a statement or situation. The whole group wears the same colour hat at the same time, so everyone is doing the same kind of thinking at the same time. The six different colours indicate different kinds of thinking: opinions and feelings (red); fact gathering (white); negative points (black); positive points (yellow); creativity and new ideas (green); planning, focus and reflection (blue).

There is no particular order in which to introduce the hats. They can be introduced one at a time. When discussing an issue, children can be asked to switch hats suddenly to change the focus of their thinking.

The hats are a visual guide to taking a new perspective. Some teachers use real hats or children can make them.

An interesting example of the use of the six hats technique is given by Wyse and Dowson.[xix] A Year 6 class were asked to think about having boys and girls in separate classes. Before trying the hats technique, the teacher asked the group to vote 'yes' or 'no'. Then, after explaining what each hat represented, she gave pairs of children a recording three-column grid sheet, each with a coloured picture of one of the hats at the top.

The children worked together to discuss the issue taking the perspectives sug-gested by each hat in turn and noting the positive and negative issues that looking through the perspective of each hat threw up. This led to a whole-class discussion and a second vote, before which the teacher asked the children to consider what everyone had said. The votes for and against the suggestion had changed, so the teacher asked whether anyone could tell the class why they had altered their opinions. The answers were variations on the following:

> "I hadn't thought before about all the other things that people said."
> "I thought it would be good to have all the boys together, because the girls are annoying, but now I think it might be boring."
> "When I looked at what I'd written, I had more points for the black hat than the yellow one, so I had to change my mind."

Here the use of the hats promotes a sort of role play and distancing from the self to see things from different points of view. This in turn leads to greater personal understanding of the issue leading children to change their minds. It is not hard to see how this technique could be adapted to other issues in any area of the curriculum.

Teaching through drama

To develop and to learn children need to be able to move beyond themselves to try out being somebody different, somebody with new skills. Students who do not learn easily may be blocked by a kind of fear of change. It is as if they are caught in the grip of a narrow self-image and cannot imagine being anything other than what it is that they think that they are. Drama, with its need to take on many roles, should be able to help here, loosening the grip of one perspective and facilitating the kind of creative reversals of perspective that dialogic creative thought depends on.

Mantle of the Expert (MoE) was developed by a drama teacher, Dorothy Heathcote,[xx] as an approach to teaching and learning that can be applied across the curriculum. In MoE there is always a client who asks the children for help. The children work together in a team to run some sort of 'enterprise'. The emphasis is on the tasks the children need to do to make their 'enterprise' successful and to help the clients. The children undertake a series of collaborative activities motivated by the client. Teamwork and communication are therefore at the centre of the learning process.

The teacher and the children in a class share responsibility for evaluating the work that gets done because the activity is always understood as a shared undertaking. The 'enterprise' stimulates and supports many tasks such as talking, listening, writing, speaking, making, designing, planning, measuring, and so on. All of these tasks can be linked in to the needs of the curriculum.

To give an example: a class of children studying the Tudor period are given roles as experts in charge of running a Tudor mansion. They prepare exhibits so that school visitors can learn about life in Tudor times.

To give another example: a group of children are in charge of running a hotel. They have to consider the needs of international visitors. This leads into work in a number of different areas such as: languages, food, finance, advertising, and so on. As their talk develops as though they are the people running the hotel so their need for specific language and knowledge increases.

Thinking at the edge

To develop creative thinking children need to become aware of voices suggesting different ways of seeing things. From Michelangelo's account it seems the voices of the angels he found trapped in the marble block were quite loud for him but for others such voices of possibilities and potentials might be distant and faint. To amplify these voices Guy Claxton has developed an approach called 'Thinking at the Edge' (TATE), based on the therapeutic practice of 'focusing'. TATE involves learning the delicate skill of attending to inner processes through which new ideas emerge. Particular forms of exploratory writing and exploratory conversation contribute to this. He argues that TATE offers a clear example of how learning dispositions may be cultivated in classrooms. Examples of the sort of activities that can help develop TATE are:

- Encouraging children to have one book with the left-hand page for drafting and doodling, and the right hand for 'the best draft so far'. Allow time and space for students to share their preliminary thoughts and experiments with each other, and to talk about what was at the back of their mind when they

were sketching, and perhaps why they decided to go with one idea instead
of another.

- Asking children to keep a book of snippets from life that are interesting but
  you don't really know why, like overheard conversations, images, quotes,
  fleeting thoughts and so on.
- Putting displays on the walls that show successive drafts of a painting, a poem,
  or a design, so that the creative process of drafting and re-drafting is made
  visible, and thereby given legitimacy, value and status.[xxi]

Conclusion

We need to teach for understanding but what is *understanding*? Understanding something new, when there is no pre-existing framework, requires a creative leap. This special
kind of 'Aha' or 'Eureka' understanding could be called creative understanding. Some
people and some children seem better at it than others. Creativity is more than just
understanding new ideas but understanding new ideas requires creativity. Teaching
for creativity in the classroom could therefore be seen as a way to teach for greater
understanding.

The chiasm idea from Merleau-Ponty suggests that the 'dialogic principle' is not
just about talk but is about a fundamental structure underlying consciousness: being
both outside-in and inside-out all at once. This, I argue, is at the origin of creativity
both in dialogues and in artistic expression. To teach for creativity then is to teach
children to move more into the space of dialogue. On the level of talk this is the
'inclusive boundary' between people in a dialogue. On a more perceptual level this
is the hinge between body and world, sentient and sensed, inside and outside. The
purpose of education for creativity is to identify less with fixed images and to identify
more with the space of possibility that underlies these images.

A dialogic classroom is a creative classroom. But what is it about interaction and
dialogues that leads to creativity? Here I find Merleau-Ponty's account of the 'chiasm'
useful. In a dialogue we are both inside ourselves looking out and outside ourselves
looking in. This capacity to be on two sides at once is the essential structure of creativity,
both creative understanding and creative production of something new. Many creative
people talk about being almost possessed by the answer that they were looking for as
if it too was looking for them and wanted to speak through them. This can sound odd,
like Michelangelo's claim that he heard angels calling him to liberate them from marble
blocks. However, it is also our everyday experience of dialogic relations when we hear
other people's voices speaking in our own heads, calling us to respond to them. The
best place to learn where to have unexpected insights then is probably in dialogues
where children can be carried beyond themselves.

In the last chapter, Chapter 3, I described various ways of teaching for creativity
that have shown themselves to be effective. Anna Craft refers to asking questions,
particularly 'What if' questions, as the engine for creating spaces of possibility in the
classroom and gives examples of ways of teaching that can promote this.[xxii] This fits
very well with the broad dialogic account of the origin of creativity that I have outlined

in this chapter. In this chapter I described even more obviously dialogic methods of teaching for creativity such as wearing different hats or taking on different roles in a drama. The point of such activities is to help children step beyond their normal boundaries in order to see things as if from the perspective of another person. Another approach from Guy Claxton, 'Thinking at the Edge' or TATE, is about learning to pay attention to elusive ideas that are often just at the limits of awareness. To me this is like learning to listen properly in a dialogue which means not only focusing on the explicit words that are being said but also reaching for the implicit meaning that can often be read in the silences between the words.

Chapter Summary

Creativity is something real. Some cultures are more creative than others and some children are more creative than others. Insight creativity of the kind exemplified in Archimedes' 'Eureka moment' takes the form of seeing things from a new perspective. The disposition for doing this is probably learnt from dialogues where we have to take the perspectives of others and see things from multiple points of view. Analysis of the experience of creativity suggests that it relies on a reversal of perspectives from the inside to the outside and the outside to the inside. The ability to do this, and so to really hear what the other is saying, begins in dialogue between people but can then be applied to fields of experience and of knowledge. Such creative learning dispositions can be taught and there are already several effective techniques for teaching them.

5   Reason

Chapter Overview

In the last three chapters I have described dialogic education as education for dialogue and I have argued that drawing children into real dialogues will help them to become not only more dialogic thinkers, able to listen and to learn from others, but also more creative thinkers. That is all very well, you might respond, but it looks as if I have been focusing on the softer more cuddly side of thinking, the dimensions of imagination and of empathy that help us see things afresh and to see things from other points of view. Creativity and empathy are important but there is also a harder side of good thinking that is about scepticism, critical analysis and rigorous argument. Children need to be helped by teachers to critically reflect on experience in order to judge between useful generalizations supported by evidence, and ungrounded prejudice. In this chapter I return to the more traditional concern of teaching thinking as being about hard critical thought in which there can be bad arguments as well as good arguments. I focus on mathematics and science examples because these are subject areas where clear reasoning and critical thinking tend to be most visible, but clear reasoning and critical thinking are needed in every area.

Talk that solves reasoning tests

In Chapter 2 I introduced the idea of dialogic thinking with an example of the talk of a group of children around a reasoning test problem. This is interesting because the test we asked the children to do in the study is one of the most reliable and rigorous tests of reasoning available: Raven's Standard Progressive Matrices. IQ is usually taken from a number of cognitive tests but if only one were to be used it would have to be the Raven's test as this correlates best with IQ and with the future educational attainment of children.[i] If you look back at the Raven's reasoning test problem example I gave in Chapter 2 you can see that the puzzle, like all the Raven's test problems, has hidden mathematical properties that the children have to work out for themselves. While the problem was apparently solved through an uncaused insight by one of the girls, this solution was then shared through a form of words: 'taking the circle out' (a version of the more general operation of subtraction). This phrase is used as a metaphor for a kind of imaginary manipulation of the puzzle. If, in imagination, you vary the top left hand square by taking the circle out you get the bottom left hand square, so it follows that if you do the same to the top right hand square and use your imagination to take the circle out you end up with the solution, an empty square (number 5). It interested me that 'taking the circle out' was a process of imagination that could not be pointed to on the page in front of them.

The phrase 'taking the circle out' is not a concept but it is an insight that is on its way to becoming a concept. This is precisely why Piaget describes the development of mathematical thinking as a progress from concrete operations, actually moving things around with your hands, perhaps taking real circles out of real squares, towards formal operations where the operations that are first acted out physically are coded in words and mathematical symbols like '+' and '−'. By using the phrase 'taking the circle out' and repeating it the children were able to see something in the puzzle that, before the words formed, was not so visible to them. Raven's Standard Progressive Matrices are called progressive because they build on each other in a series of similar problems. Tara gave a label to her initial perception of how to solve the puzzle: 'taking the circle out', and helped the children carry this insight forward and use it to solve other similar problems where variations of the same phrase occurred such as 'taking the square out' or 'putting the diamond in'.

As well as looking at particular groups solving particular problems I also analysed how the talk of children changed in general over the period of three months when we were teaching them 'Thinking Together': that is, I compared their talk about the reasoning test test we gave them initially (the pre-test) with their talk about the reasoning test that we gave them to do afterwards (the post-test). In general I found that in the pre-test there was a lot more pointing at the page and that in the post-test there was a lot more referring to phrases like 'taking the circle out'. There was a general shift from the physical to the verbal. This shift in the way that they were talking correlated with their getting right more of the reasoning test problems.[ii] It seems that our Thinking Together programme had led them to uncover the hidden invisible structures of the puzzles and make them visible in words so that they could refer to them and discuss them. They were still in the same physical context, of course, and they could still point at the puzzle in the test booklet open on the table in front of them and say 'No, cos look . . . ' and jab down with their finger on the page. It was just that, in addition to this, they now had an extra layer of reality to refer to and they could now also say things like 'I see that but look here, on this one they have taken the circle out see and if you take the circle out on this one then you get that . . . '.

I think that this story of how the children solved reasoning test problems by creating a shared language together offers a model of cognitive development in general. Looking at cognitive development as if from the outside it appears that children start off as physical bodies interacting with physical objects in physical space. But they are different from other physical objects because they have an inside. From a very early age children are also in dialogic relationships that enable them to feel what others feel and to see things as if from others' perspectives. These relationships draw them into dialogues that are initially physical and then become verbal, creating a second space of language like a second skin. Unlike the first animal skin, the cultural skin of language is shared with others.

Talking about counting: is 5 + 3 the same as 3 + 5?

If you ask a 6-year-old: what is 5 add 3? they will probably first count out five fingers and then count on three, opening each finger in turn saying '6','7','8'. then if you ask them: what is 3 add 5? they will probably do the whole operation again counting out three fingers and then counting on another five fingers to find that the answer is, once again, 8.

The children are counting correctly and getting the answers right but they have not understood that, in arithmetic, 5 + 3 is the same as 3 + 5. If you ask them about numbers and operations like addition they understand this in terms of the procedures they have to do like counting on their fingers but they do not understand the abstract concept of a number or of addition. How can we help them to move from procedures to a more conceptual understanding?

When I talked to maths educators about this and similar problems in early mathematics I realized that the issue was similar in some respects to the problem that the children had faced in solving the reasoning tests together. To solve the reasoning tests the children had to see invisible relationships and give them a label. In moving from physical space to a verbal space they were moving to a more conceptual understanding of the mathematical relationships hidden in the puzzles. If Exploratory Talk helped children to solve reasoning tests then perhaps it would help children to understand some of the basic relationships of arithmetic, particularly the concept of 'commutativity' or that 5 + 3 is just another way of saying 3 + 5.

Mathematics education specialist Carol Murphy and I, with other colleagues at the University of Exeter, put together a project combining Exploratory Talk and mathematics to see if talking together would help young children shift up a level in their understanding of mathematics concepts. We are only halfway through the project but the results so far look promising.

One teacher we are working with, Susan, taught her class of 6 and 7-year-olds the ground rules for Exploratory Talk and then asked them to work together in groups of three solving a simple form of magical square. They were given the numbers 3, 2 and 1 on cards and asked to arrange them in a 3 by 3 grid so that every row and column added up to the same.

1	2	3
2	3	1
3	1	2

Figure 5.1 Magic square

In one group we video-recorded two of the group, Jack and Amy, worked industri-ously arranging numbers and counting them out while a girl called Judy just watched them.

> 'Two, three and one,' Jack counted on his fingers, 'that's six'.
> 'One, three and two,' Amy counted on her fingers, 'six'.

They were succeeding at the task, finding the way in which the numbers could be used to make all the rows and columns add up to the same total, but they did not seem to realize that $3 + 2 + 1$ was the same as $1 + 2 + 3$ and the same as $2 + 1 + 3$ etc. Judy sucked her finger looking on, then said: 'They are all adding up to six, look they are all six'. She said it quite loud and they certainly heard her but they carried on counting out numbers in rows and columns as if they had not really understood her point.

When Susan the teacher came around to this group she praised them for arranging the numbers correctly to form a magic square and emphasized the point that Judy had seen, that if you use only the three number cards '1', '2' and '3' then the answer is always 6 regardless of the order. She concluded by saying, 'So, there is no need to keep counting on your fingers, you know that they add up to six'.

The principle of three

This group had not been using all the talk ground rules but the collaboration itself seemed to spark an insight in Judy and prepared the ground for teaching commuta-tivity. It is interesting that out of the three children she was the one least involved in the procedure of the task but was the one looking on. There is an old saying 'Two is company, three's a crowd'. In groups of three, two children will often happily support each other in doing the task as they see it while one is left out slightly. This knowledge that three is an awkward number often leads teachers to be resistant to the idea of grouping in threes. But the experience of the Thinking Together project shows that three is the best number for developing thinking. The child left feeling a bit spare in the group is often the one who challenges the others to think more about what they are doing.

Invoking the absent addressee

In the example above the children could 'count on' but they did not really understand the concept of addition. This illustrates a general issue for education; how can we move people from knowing how to do something, a knowledge that depends on the particular task and tools, to understanding the same thing conceptually so that they are free to play with the ideas? The big question for education is how can the knowledge that children have procedurally, be translated into more conscious understanding? For example, how can knowledge of how to count on your fingers be translated into real understanding of mathematical operations like addition? The psychologist Annette

Karmiloff-Smith refers to this as the problem of 'representational redescription'. When the children can only add up by counting on their fingers they represent addition in one way, through a physical procedure, but when they understand that $3 + 5$ is the same as $5 + 3$ it is because they have represented addition in another way through concepts that can be expressed in words or symbols. Karmiloff-Smith was a student of the hugely influential Swiss psychologist Jean Piaget whom I described in Chapter 1 as having a rather mechanical view of the mind. It is perhaps not surprising then that she argues that 'representational redescription' occurs in some sort of internal mechanism of the individual mind. But what we see time and again in primary classrooms is the shift from procedural to conceptual understanding occurring in dialogues. It is other people, especially teachers, who call us to reflect on what we are doing and to understand it in order to explain it. Even when, as with the case of Judy described above, insight does not come directly as a response to a question but in a moment of reflection, that reflection takes the form of seeing the problem as if afresh through new eyes or from another person's point of view.

The lever that shifts children, and all of us, from a limited procedural understanding to a broader conceptual understanding is not mechanical but dialogic: it is not a cogwheel clicking into place, it is the gaze of the other that leads us to understand. Insight often stems from an internal gaze seeing the same things differently so that they make sense for the first time. But to see things differently is to see things as if from the perspective of another person. That individual insight is made possible because first we are led by dialogues to see things through the eyes of others. Because a dialogue is part of a relationship we feel impelled to explain ourselves to the other. In reflecting on our actions so as to explain them to others we can be led to understand them for the first time for ourselves.

The other we address in dialogue is not always a real other, sometimes it is simply the idea of another person. In fact even in dialogues with a real other person we often find ourselves trying to explain clearly as if for a third person, a witness, someone who will understand us even if the person we are talking to is too dense or too self-interested to listen properly. The crucial role that the absent addressee can play in precipitating a shift in understanding can be seen clearly in some data sent to me for analysis from an American primary classroom.[iii]

In the data a group of four children had been told to make a graph but had not been told how to make it. They had been growing plants as a class and had measured each plant's height each day. One of the children, Angelina, wanted to write down all the observation data in cells linked to each plant name. She had not really understood how a graph can help display information. Julia and Tom argued with her that they should map the height of the plants on one axis against the days on the other axis. They argued for a long time even turning the graph paper around so that they could literally see it from each other's point of view. At one point in the video it is possible to see that Angelina changes her mind quite dramatically and concedes to the argument of the others. How does this happen? She precedes her change of mind by listening intently to Julia then turning her head away from Julia a little, as if for a moment of private thought, then she lifts her head slowly with a long drawn out 'Ohhh!' and her eyes widen as her mouth opens into the 'O' shape which is at the same time a kind of smile.

Is it the argument that Julia has just given that enables her to see things so differently? Before Angelina's conversion, Will had just said:

> 'That's what you're telling them with the graph – that's why we're making the graph!'

And then Julia had added:

> 'We're saying: "It's day nineteen – how is it going?"'

As she said this she turned a little to the side and made an exaggerated welcoming gesture with her hand drawing in an imaginary viewer from outside to look at the graph.

There was something at stake for Angelina in not changing her mind as she had invested time in her arguments and she wanted to be right, yet she found herself led, almost despite herself, to see Julia's point of view. The quality of the relationships in the group is crucial to this achievement of unforced agreement. The ground rules operating in this group meant that challenges were responded to with reasons, not with a breakdown of communication, and that changes of mind were possible (although this was touch and go at times as they got quite angry with each other).

It seems that Angelina's change of mind here did not stem from any abstract logic so much as from a shift in perspective to see the graph from a projected future point of view – the point of view of the future viewer of the graph referred to and brought into the discussion by Julia and Will. This change of mind is preceded by the gesture of drawing in the alternative perspective, the future viewer.[iv]

There is something very resonant about this example for me. This invocation of an absent future addressee – the person who will finally read what you are writing or understand your thoughts – seems to speak of something at the heart of all thinking. Sitting here now at my desk in Exeter University I am thinking hard, arguing all the time, struggling with alternative ways of presenting ideas, but there is nobody here with me. My 'thinking' is not an individual affair but nor is it a dialogue with a physically present other person. It is a dialogue with you, the projected reader of my text, or the absent future addressee. Somewhere in my educational journey I must have learnt to engage in such dialogues with an absent future perspective. It is a strange skill, talking to someone virtual, a silent witness, who is not there now but might be one day. Yet this is a skill that everyone who learns to think and to write and to succeed at education must acquire somehow. This is how we are able to convert our narrow, particular and situated vision into an understanding that is more general and that is transferable to other contexts. This is how we learn to reason.

Even as I make this claim I can hear an objection from a possible future reader: 'But surely you are just communicating and persuading when you write? For me thinking is not just about persuading other people, when I think I don't use words at all.' This is a good challenge. In the example of children solving a reasoning test problem that I offer at the beginning of Chapter 2 it is possible to see that Tara solves the problem alone as a kind of way of seeing the problem (the light of understanding almost literally dawns on her face) and then she tries to share this in words, failing at first and only finding the right words the second time that she tries. I get this effect as well when I am writing. Sometimes I am choosing words carefully to persuade an imagined reader but at other times I stop writing altogether, sit back and think. When I am really thinking there are fragments of signs and words and pictures in my mind, but I am not thinking in a way that would make sense to anyone else. At times like that we might want to say, 'I am thinking it through for myself'. But actually what we often think of as individual thinking is really a kind of inner dialogue in which we see things not only from different perspectives but also from a sort of distance, taking the perspective of an 'other' that is not in any way defined. I think that inner otherness that comes into play when we are really thinking for ourselves is a virtual version of the real others who first call us to think. This inner other may also be the key to understanding reason as I explain in the next section.

Reason as dialogue with the infinite other that always escapes from us

So far in this book I have given examples that stress the need for creative lateral thinking, thinking that steps sidewise to see things from new perspectives. But there is also sometimes a vertical direction in thinking, thinking that gets a clearer vision, not just a different vision but a better and truer vision. In Chapter 2 I argued that we should understand thinking, following Heidegger, as a kind of dialogue but not as a dialogue with Being, but rather as a dialogue with what Levinas called 'the infinite other'. I think that this idea that thinking is called forth by an infinite other can help us to understand the vertical direction in thinking.[v]

Infinity sounds grand but is actually an everyday experience. I explain infinity to children as 'Think of the biggest number you possibly can and then add one. However big the number is, you can always add one, that is infinity'. In a dialogue it is also true that whatever position you reach there can always be a further response or interpretation. One way of thinking about how infinity might enter into dialogues is a simple classroom experiment with two mirrors set up parallel to each other so that each reflects the light from the other. If you use plexiglass mirrors you can easily cut a hole in one mirror and look through. What you see is an infinite regression of mirrors inside mirrors inside mirrors. If you place a small object between the two mirrors that too can be seen an infinite number of times getting smaller and smaller as it retreats into the distance. Real dialogues all have this same potential for infinity that comes from mutual reflection. Of course we are not like mirrors reflecting the same image back to each other. Even if we try really hard to reflect what we hear from people straight back to them we will change it by expressing it in our own words. Human dialogue is always creative and every dialogue has the potential to be infinitely creative.

In a dialogue we might start just trying to persuade the other person but in doing so we listen to our own arguments as if from an outside point of view. If you go back to the example of solving a reasoning test problem in Chapter 2, this effect can be seen in the talk of Tara. In the post-test example Tara suggests a solution and Perry asks her to explain what she means and, in the very act of explaining it, she changes her mind. Perry calls her to think but he does not give arguments to make her change her mind, it is simply her own awareness of her position that makes her change her mind. In looking at her idea again she looks at it as if through another's eyes. This is the witness position, or the 'third' position, that Bakhtin writes is generated by every dialogue. Words in dialogues are not just aimed at specific others, they also become aimed at a sort of otherness in general. If you try to pin down this witness position in order to dialogue with it you will find that another witness position is automatically generated. The witness position is the addressee of thought but it is an unpindownable addressee that Bakhtin calls the super-addressee.[vi] Because it can never be grasped, because it always runs away from us when we try to catch it, the super-addressee can justly be called the infinite other.

This analysis of infinity in dialogues enables us to understand more clearly how children learn to reason. First they are called to explain themselves in dialogues with specific others. In the act of doing so they become drawn into a dialogue with a third position that every dialogue generates, the position of the super-addressee or the infinite other. While dialogue with specific others can be about persuasion and who gets to have the final answer and write it down on the answer sheet, dialogue with the infinite other is about truth.

In Chapter 2 I described the development into thinking of groups of children solving reasoning tests together, in terms of learning to enter more deeply into dialogue and to identify with the space of dialogue itself. This development is not just about dialogue with individuals, it is also about engaging more deeply in dialogue with the infinite other. This kind of identity, identifying with being in relationship with the infinite other, is never static because, of course, the infinite other is not some kind of thing but more like a constant call to go beyond your prejudices and assumptions in order to see yourself as if from the outside. Another way of putting this is, acquiring a passion for truth.

Two models of cognitive development

Vygotsky writes about how children's experiences lead to the formation of ideas that are fuzzy complexes, informed by words but still embedded in the contexts in which they are experienced (see Figure 5.2). Perhaps the idea of 'taking the circle out' which children developed for themselves to solve a problem described in Chapter 2 is a fuzzy context-dependent complex of this kind. Full concepts, on the other hand, concepts like subtraction, are logical and live in the pre-existing language of the culture. If education works it is a kind of negotiation or dialogue between teachers and children in which their emergent ideas are grafted onto pre-existing concepts. Full concepts, Vygotsky writes, exist in relation to other concepts in a logical conceptual system where every term is defined by every other term.[vii]

This account is insightful in many ways but it suggests a one-way hierarchical progress in which the initial 'participatory' thinking of children is overcome and re-placed by more abstract and logical thinking. The focus of this and similar accounts is on the development of explicit rationality. Creative thinking is harder to explain on this model. Although dialogue enters into this account it is just as a means to the achievement of a monological (single-voiced) conceptual system.

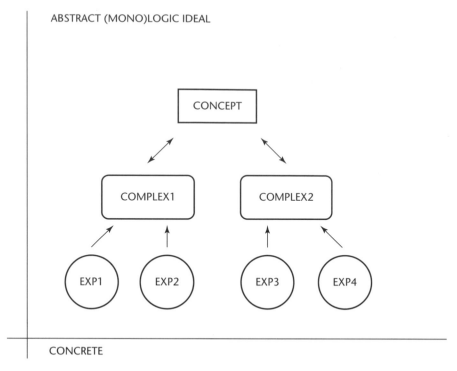

Figure 5.2 Vygotsky's model of conceptual development

An alternative more genuinely dialogic account of conceptual development would suggest that concepts do not replace experience. Thought always remains participatory and metaphorical. Concepts are always fuzzy and they are always temporary provisional staging posts, like eddies in a stream, where experiences are brought together in dialogues (see Figure 5.3). In fact concepts are not solid things at all but more like perspectives on reality achieved in a dialogue and then given a marker in language.

Think of the way in which the children described in Chapter 2 saw a pattern in the puzzle and managed to give it a reference with the phrase 'taking the circle out'. This phrase refers to that way of seeing the puzzle and has to be reanimated to have meaning. In dialogues the participatory voices are never completely overcome but remain and can be recovered later if needed. Conceptual development is not about experience being drawn up into a pre-existing logical system but about experience being organized by seeing as if from the perspective of others and ultimately as if from the perspective of the witness position or the ideal of the infinite other that emerges from every dialogue.

What is science and how to teach it?

A distressingly large number of people still seem to think that science is all about facts. Science is a shared enquiry: a continuous dialogue with no final right answers.

Figure 5.3   Whirl of dialogues

Much of what we thought we knew for certain a hundred years ago has been radically reinterpreted by later voices in the dialogue. It is not that Newton was wrong exactly but Einstein, Bohr and others showed that he had only seen a small part of a much bigger picture. It is a safe bet that what we think we know now will also be radically reinterpreted in the future. In this context it is wise to teach not only the provisional conclusions of scientific dialogues but also the process. Teaching science is engaging children in the process of collaborative enquiry informed by evidence and open to scrutiny.

Some people think science can be distinguished from other areas of shared enquiry by its rigorous scientific method. Rigour is certainly important as is openness about methods so that they can be examined and tested by others, but there is no fixed scientific method. The history of science shows a tremendous creativity about devising new methods to explore new problems. The only fixed 'method' is that of argumentation. After creatively coming up with a hypothesis, scientists are often extraordinarily ingenious in devising a way to test this hypothesis. But creative experimentation is only the beginning, scientists then have to argue for the significance of their findings, linking available evidence to a theory. If the argument works then there is convergence and consensus for a while but experience shows that however convinced everyone is, they may be wrong and the arguments that they used to convince themselves may all be challenged later.

Science is desperately important for our society but what is most important about it are not the apparent facts that it offers nor the methods that particular scientists use:

what is most important is the creative and rigorously critical thinking that underlies it. The best way to teach science well is to teach it as a process of shared enquiry characterized by creativity, criticality and open-mindedness. This should include rigorous public argumentation where claims are ultimately grounded on evidence that comes from shared experience.

Teaching reasoning

Accountable talk

Above I described the reasoning in one classroom as being motivated by a dialogue with a future addressee; that is, the outside person who was going to have to make sense of the children's graph when they had finished it. A version of this idea is that we are writing or working for a community of enquiry. This is the community of scientists who might come to accept our ideas in the future even if they do not understand them right now. Bakhtin wrote that different cultures and times generate their own image of the super-addressee and for some the super-addressee was the idea of the future community of scientists.[viii]

A similar understanding lies behind accountable talk, which is a practical approach to teaching reason in the classroom championed by Lauren Resnick. In accountable talk children listen carefully to one another, build on each other's ideas, and ask each other questions aimed at clarifying or expanding ideas. They make concessions and partial concessions and provide reasons when they disagree or agree. They also extend or elaborate someone else's argument, or ask someone for elaboration of their idea. Apparently teachers only need a small number of 'talk moves' in order to create this kind of talk community. These are as follows:

Table 5.1 Talk move action for accountable talk

Talk move action	An example
Revoicing.	'So let me see if I've understood you. Are you saying . . . ?' (With time for students to accept or reject the new formulation.)
Asking students to restate someone else's reasoning.	'Can you repeat what he just said in your own words?'
Asking students to apply their own reasoning to someone else's reasoning.	'Do you agree or disagree and why?'
Prompting students for further participation.	'Would someone like to add on?'
Asking students to explicate their reasoning.	'Why do you think that?' or 'How did you arrive at that answer?' or 'Say more about that.'
Challenge or counter-example.	'Is this always true?' or 'Can you think of any examples that would not work?'

Children take to the 'accountability to community' moves easily and create new more rational norms of classroom talk. The idea is that they become accountable to each other but also to the larger community, particularly to the norms that exist for reason and for knowledge. However, Resnick and colleagues write, for this approach to succeed it is very important that the children are given interesting and complex ideas to talk and argue about. Teachers who have implemented these discourse strategies have shifted away from simple questions and one-word answers and opened up the classroom talk to multiple positions, complex pathways and uncertainty of outcome.

The same sort of questions and 'talk moves' are found in Philosophy for Children and also in Thinking Together. However, Accountable Talk is an independent movement with good evidence for its efficacy in promoting better reasoning and also better learning. This success brings out what is of most central importance in all classroom dialogue: responsibility to the addressee even if they take the absent and abstract form of a 'community'.[ix]

There are several other successful dialogic approaches to teaching maths and science. For example, the Thinking Together approach that I outlined in Chapter 2 has been applied successfully to teaching science in primary classrooms, and so has teaching informal argumentation.[x]

Thinking together

When we applied the Thinking Together approach to science we found that it was very important to create the right kind of activities that would support the children's thinking and talking but also support achieving understanding of issues within the primary curriculum. One method we used a lot was something that I called IDRF activities supported by computer software. IDRF is a development out of the more typical teacher-led exchange structure of IRF: Initiation, Response, Feedback. An example might be:

I. Teacher: What is the boiling point of water?

R. Child: 100 degrees centigrade.

F. Teacher: Well done!

This way of using questions to test knowledge is common in schools but has been criticized for not allowing space for children to think. The IDRF teaching exchange structure adds an extra D for Dialogue element in the exchange. An example is given in my book with Lyn Dawes, *Thinking and Learning with ICT*,[xi] where a science simulation programme enables children to test out how sound is carried through a range of materials, but before they are allowed to design and run experiments another bit of software called 'Talking Bug' (a ladybird that talks and prompts the children to talk which I made myself) challenges them:

I. Talking Bug (TB): In this lab you can test how well four different materials block out sound. Which material do you predict will be the best at blocking out a high-pitched sound, like a whistle? Talk together to decide and say your reasons why before you click on a button.

D. The three children in the group then discuss this question at length giving a range of answers and reasons for their answers. Finally they agree that it must be metal because this is 'the hardest'.

R. One child, with the agreement of the group, selects the answer metal from a multiple choice menu.

F. The TB encourages them to check this out with the simulation and they find it was in fact cork. The TB knows they got it wrong and asks them to talk together to figure out why they got it wrong. At this point the teacher turns up and talks them through why cork absorbs more sound than metal due to its lower density. This is also the theme of her plenary.

Some might say that this activity is not really very dialogic because there is a right answer that the teacher knows and that the software knows. But the dialogic element of teaching for dialogue is maintained by teaching the ground rules of talk and focusing on talk in the lessons. This enables them to hold more than one perspective together in tension in their dialogue and in their dialogue with the computer. This kind of teaching allows the children to articulate their own views and is far more likely to lead to sparks of understanding than simply telling them the right way to think.

We tested the learning impact of the Thinking Together approach in science and mathematics over a year. The sound insulation lesson described above was one of many activities most of which used widely available software. The common thread was that all of the activities supported IDRF exchanges of the kind described above, and that the children understood the nature and purpose of using joint ground rules to talk together. This approach was found to stimulate thinking together through dialogue in contexts that supported the teacher's specific learning intentions for science and mathematics. Six target classes were matched with six similar 'control' classes in other schools. Both the experimental and control classes were given a test of scientific understanding in the topics covered in Year 5 of the UK curriculum at the beginning and at the end of the school year. The questions we used were taken from optional SATs published by the UK government. Statistical analysis showed that the difference in scores in favour of the target classes was highly significant.[xii]

Concept cartoons

The Thinking Together approach works well in conjunction with 'Concept Cartoons'[xiii] in which cartoon children suggest alternative ideas about a puzzle with a science theme. For example, how do batteries work? Is it because they contain electricity which comes out of each end along the wires and meets in the bulb in the middle? Or because they make a spark which lights the bulb? The group discuss these and their own ideas to reach a joint, reasoned decision about what they think. This may or may not be the 'right' answer, but the talk allows the teacher to discern and address their children's misconceptions. It is then possible to address these with specifically focused further activities.

Puppets

The people behind 'Concept Cartoons', Brenda Keogh and Stuart Naylor, have now developed an approach to teaching and learning science with puppets which is particularly effective at engaging young children. The approach involves two large handheld puppets that are used to introduce scientific concepts and at the same time pose a problem for the children to solve. For example, the puppet might have lost keys down a grating and cannot get into his house. How can he get them back? What seems like a simple problem becomes a difficult one as the children discover how hard it is to retrieve the keys. Discussions ensue as the children come up with ideas. This is where the concept of magnetism can be introduced and the children can be led to discover together how this can solve the problem.

Research findings so far suggest that children find it easier to learn with puppets, treating them as if they are real characters and responding positively to the scientific problems they face. Like the use of software, puppets are a way of introducing problems to talk about that enables the teacher to step out of the way. This is normally quite important as the teacher is normally treated as an authority making it hard to stimulate discussion, especially when the question has a right answer and the teacher knows it. Puppets work especially well when they are involved in a story where they have a problem to solve. Children will want to help the puppets by solving the problem. At the end of the story the children can talk directly to the puppet about how they think they can solve the problem.[xiv]

An evaluation study was carried out with sixteen teachers of children aged 7–11 years in schools in London and Manchester. This found that where puppets were used in science lessons there was:

- more argumentation and fewer recall responses with more opportunities to develop thinking about science.
- more children's talk with reasons.
- a change in teachers' questioning style towards offering more opportunities for thinking.
- more teacher use of argumentation and less time spent on the delivery of information.

Many might find it odd that puppets should make such a difference but this finding fits very well with the dialogic theory of teaching for thinking and creativity that I have outlined in this book. Learning to think, especially learning to think in subject areas like science, is about engaging in dialogue with cultural voices. Although learning to think starts with dialogue between embodied voices it then spins off into dialogue with ideas and even with absent ideals like the future addressee or the infinite other. Software, like my 'Talking Bug', cartoon characters with speech bubbles and talking puppets can all serve to facilitate the transition from a fixed identity experience of voices to the more flexible and multiple voices of positions in dialogic space. This is the space where the dance of ideas is to be found.

How do you know that the Earth is not flat? Prove it!

Stephen Toulmin introduced a description of what he called 'informal logic'. His terminology such as 'warrant' suggests that his perspective was influenced by the kind of argumentation used by lawyers to persuade the judge or jury in courtrooms. His account breaks argumentation down into the following moves:[xv]

- a *claim* states the standpoint or conclusion, for example: 'The Earth is flat, not a round ball'.
- the *data* are the facts or opinions that the claim is based on, for example: 'The Earth looks flat'.
- the *warrant* provides the justification for using the data as support for the claim, for example: 'If the Earth was round the horizon would be more curved than it is'.
- optionally, the *backing* provides specific information supporting the warrant, for example: 'When you go out to sea on a calm day the horizon looks flat'.
- a *qualifier* adds a degree of certainty to the conclusion, indicating the degree of force which the arguers attribute to a claim, for example: 'However, I am not sure how curved it would have to be before it would look curved'.
- exceptions to the claim are expressed by a *rebuttal*, for example: 'People claim to have travelled around the Earth but I think it is shaped like a round plate and those people probably got lost and travelled around the edge of the plate'.

In itself this is not a dialogic account of argumentation, it is just a grammar of argument that does not look at relationships and responses. However, studies have found that versions of this scheme can offer a shared vocabulary for reasoning in science. All areas of science can be taught by reconstructing the arguments around new ideas or discoveries. Does the moon shine with its own light? Is the Earth flat? By not focusing on the facts but on the arguments behind the facts science is taught as a dynamic and continuing process of shared enquiry.[xvi]

Conclusion

In this chapter I explored the issue of teaching reasoning that is critical and rigorous as well as creative. I gave examples of how understanding in mathematics education requires that children learn to take the perspective of the other. I argued that, while taking the perspective of specific others expands the space of dialogue with more points of view, there is also a vertical dimension to engaging in dialogue. This verticality comes from the silent witness in every dialogue. Children begin to reason in order to explain themselves to their classmates but then get drawn into arguing for the sake of truth. It is not possible to make an argument addressed to a specific other without at the same time listening to it as if from the point of view of a non-specific other. This taking the perspective of the other to oneself is the beginning of internal thought. I argued that the best way to understand this direction of reason is as a kind of dialogue with otherness itself, or the infinite other. This 'other' is not a real position that one can reach but rather a constant moving beyond any position in order to reflect on it and question it. While of course it may be useful to teach rules of good argument in specific situations, what really characterizes reason and science is not a set of rules but the passion for truth that comes from identifying with a relationship with the infinitely other. All this means is that, whoever you think you are and whatever you think you know, you are always willing to question yourself and to see yourself as if from the outside. More than that, a dialogic person is not frightened to be proved wrong but positively enjoys the prospect of learning something new.

There are many tried and tested ways to teach reasoning and argumentation in science and mathematics. Some of the most effective ways like accountable talk and the use of puppets take into account the essentially dialogic nature of reason. Accountable talk motivates children to take responsibility for the quality of their reasoning in the light of the community of scientists and researchers, which is ultimately an appeal to a future consensus of the community. Puppets help to present scientific dialogues in ways that are distanced from specific others. This is motivating and helps draw children out of the idea that dialogues are dialogues with specific others and into the dialogue with cultural voices that are positions in dialogic space. The approach of teaching children some moves in informal arguments using the Toulmin scheme and then approaching every topic in science through argument already has a good track record. All of the approaches to reason discussed in this chapter focus on science and mathematics as a process of open-ended shared enquiry characterized by the use of evidence to support public arguments.

In the new primary curriculum evolution will be taught. It is hard to understand the full significance of Darwin's view that evolution occurs through random variation and selection of genes unless this view is contrasted to the alternative proposed by Lamarck that evolution occurs through the inheritance of individual characteristics acquired during a lifetime. Did giraffes grow long necks by stretching up to the trees? Or was it that giraffes with longer necks lived to maturity more often than their shorter necked cousins and so had more babies who carried on their 'long neck gene'? What evidence do we need to decide between these two accounts? How did Darwin win the argument?

Where there is content to teach the best way to teach it is as a field of dialogue. This way the children learn the positions in the debate and the argument moves at the same time as they acquire the content knowledge that they also need.

Chapter Summary

Empathy and creativity are important to good thinking in every area since they allow us to see things from other people's point of view and from new points of view. However, they are only half the story of good thinking. Rigorous critical thinking which applies judgement to select the best answers to questions is also important in every area. In this chapter I focused on dialogic teaching in maths and science in contexts where there are right answers that the teacher knows in advance. I argued that conceptual development can be understood dialogically even in rigorously logical and abstract subjects like mathematics. And I argued, with illustrations of good practice, that the best way to teach these areas is as a process of shared enquiry. In this way the children learn to think, role-playing being real scientists or mathematicians, at the same time as they learn important content area knowledge.

6 Thinking through the curriculum

Written with the help of Steve Higgins

Chapter Overview

In the last few chapters I have explored what thinking is and what creativity is and how they can be taught through dialogic education. In the last chapter I outlined a strategy for teaching science content by drawing children into a field of dialogue. In this chapter I present the strategies approach to teaching thinking through the curriculum. This was developed by Steve Higgins and colleagues at Newcastle University some time ago and has proved very useful in promoting more reflection within the curriculum. In this chapter I argue that what really works about the strategies approach is the way that it opens a space for dialogue. Often this is a limited or bounded space inducting children into a 'field of dialogue' and into the use of particular dialogue strategies. Teaching content in a way that promotes thinking about that content and an ability to be creative with that content could also be paraphrased as teaching for understanding.

An infusion of herbs in a kettle of hot water will enrich all the water, adding colour, flavour and fragrance. The idea behind 'infusing' teaching thinking into the normal school curriculum is that it will enrich the learning in a similar way. While infusion can be described as a teaching thinking skills approach it could also be described as being simply about good teaching or 'teaching for understanding'. Thinking through the curriculum is an approach to teaching and learning which offers principles to guide teaching and strategies to promote thinking in any subject area. These strategies are often good ways of opening dialogues, breaking down complex ideas into manageable activities and offering practice in specific thinking skills.

The teacher of a lively class of 5 and 6-year-olds points to some pictures of animals arranged on the interactive whiteboard at the front of the class in a triangle shape.

- A frog, a duck and a hen. Which could be the odd one out and why?
    The duck, David, yes – why do you say that? Because it has a long neck? It does
    have a longer neck than the frog and the hen – that's right...
- The hen, Stephanie? Because ...?
    Of course, it doesn't live in water, does it? That's a good reason. The other two
    live in and around water.
- Can anyone think of another reason why the hen is the odd one out?
    Yes, Susan, that's another good reason – it does not have webbed feet. The frog
    and the duck are similar because they both have webbed feet.
- Another reason?
    The hen because it is facing the wrong way? What do you mean the wrong
    way, Robin? Oh I see, it is facing the other way from the frog and the duck.
- The frog is the odd one out is it, Nathan, and what is your reason? Because it does
    not have a beak – and it is not a bird – that is good thinking – you are right,
    birds have beaks, but frogs don't.
- Feathers – it doesn't have feathers either, good one Paul. Birds have feathers too.
- Have you got any ideas, Mark? The frog? Why is that? Because it lays eggs? But
    don't ducks and hens lay eggs too? Ahhh, but not in soft shells – I see what
    you mean. A frog's eggs are different from a bird's eggs aren't they?

This activity is suitable for whole-class interaction, but here there are a range of possible answers each of which need to be justified with reasons. The young children mainly give answers related to their science understanding (particularly in terms of variation and classification of living things and their understanding of animals and their habitats). When they think of a new or different idea you can see their enthusiasm to join in. The teacher can learn about their current level of science knowledge from their responses. Some of them can talk about birds and they have an implicit understanding of habitats.

But above all she is modelling reasoning and communicating her enthusiasm for open-ended thinking. For example, she sounded disappointed at first with Mark's suggestion. But Mark got a chance to elaborate on what he meant and her obvious pleasure at his more subtle distinction gave Mark a sense of achievement. He was clearly able to generalize from his particular knowledge of frogs and birds, about general categories and similarities and differences.

This is an example of what can be called a powerful pedagogical strategy.[i] It aims to be a catalyst to support the interaction between the teacher and the class in order to promote thinking in any subject area. In this particular strategy, Odd-One-Out, a teacher presents pupils with three ideas either as words, pictures or symbols, such as a picture of a hen, a frog and a duck in the example above. Pupils then choose one of the items to be the 'odd one out' and they have to give a reason to justify their choice. A typical response might be that the frog is the odd one out because it does not have a beak or feathers, or it is not a bird, or is an amphibian depending on their knowledge and understanding of classification in science.[ii]

This strategy is now very widely used in primary education. It was developed by a team involved in initial teacher education and continuing professional development at Newcastle University in the 1990s. A group of former teachers and researchers started gathering and creating together generic, flexible and creative strategies for use with the teachers and with the teachers in training that they were working with. Their idea was to make lessons more challenging and more likely to stimulate understanding. These strategies are different from more general interaction tools, such as collaboration techniques like Think Pair Share, in that they also provide a structure for engaging with teaching content. For example we saw science being dealt with above.

Odd-One-Out

The simple strategy described above can be applied in almost any area of the curriculum. Wherever the Odd One Out strategy is introduced it provides a stimulus to the act of comparing and it mobilizes questions using key concepts such as *same*, *quality*, *relation*, *important* and *class*.

An example in primary mathematics might be to give the class three numbers arranged in a triangle on a whiteboard and ask which is the odd one out and why? (See Figure 6.1.)

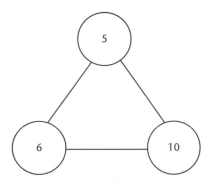

Figure 6.1 Odd One Out in maths

Is 10 the odd one out as the only double-digit number? Is 5 the odd one out as the only odd number? Or is 6 the odd one out as the only number not a multiple of 5? In discussion it might also emerge that 5 is the only prime number or number divisible only by itself. Are any of the differences more important than any others or are they all on the same level?

In this way children are led to explore the properties of numbers and their relationships in an open-ended way. An elaboration is to write on the board – which could be an interactive whiteboard – some actual relationships between the numbers as well as their peculiarities (see Figure 6.2).

Progression in this sort of activity not only involves increasing complexity of subject matter but also increasing internalization of relevant concepts and questions by students. So, students should know that comparing can be a key to understanding because they know they have learned from the Odd One Out activity. In future they should be looking for opportunities to learn by comparing. They will also know the kinds of

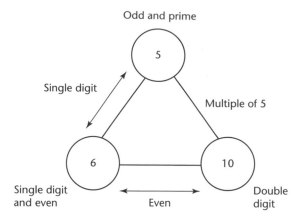

Figure 6.2 Odd One Out for number awareness

clusters of questions that the act of comparing requires such as: In what ways are these things the *same*? What *qualities* are the *same*? What are the most *important similarities*? Are the things *different* in more ways than they are the *same*? Can we *measure* the *qualities* of *sameness* or *difference*? How do we come to know of the qualities the things share – by *observation*, *assumption* or *inference*?

These kinds of considerations will be the subject of the plenary or 'de-briefing' sessions that follow these kinds of activities.

Banned

In a strategy called Banned learners focus on vocabulary and meanings by defining key ideas in a subject or topic without using common words or phrases. In this way it is similar to Odd One Out in that it deals with concepts and specific vocabulary. Banned is like the party game Taboo where teams have to describe words without being able to use those which most naturally come to mind. For example, try to describe a pizza without using the words 'round', 'flat', 'tomato', 'cheese', 'dough' or 'Italy'. Originally devised as a party game, in this version teams design sets of cards to play against each other and therefore become engaged in thinking collaboratively in their groups to devise clear definitions (in order to work out which words should be banned or made taboo) to make it difficult for the opposing group. As a pedagogical strategy it helps to develop vocabulary and the use of analogies and knowledge of specific examples.

Setting targets

Many of us will be very familiar, perhaps too familiar, with the strategy of setting criteria for success and then assessing whether or not these criteria have been met. This sort of feedforward and feedback strategy is widely used as a management tool – sometimes in a coercive way. But when criteria are discussed and negotiated, they provide people with a set of standards to aim at and to assess their efforts against. The common metaphor of criteria as 'targets' can be used to develop another thinking strategy for learners.

In one rural first school the children were introduced to the idea of criteria with a simple exercise. The teachers first asked the question: 'What makes a good pet?'. After pair-work, brainstorming and whole-class discussion three criteria emerged: 'easy to feed', 'doesn't bite' and 'not too big'. The teacher then drew a diagram of a target on the whiteboard (see Figure 6.3) with three circles, outer ring for 'meets one criteria', middle ring for 'meets two criteria' and bulls-eye for 'meets all three criteria'. The children quickly discovered that even a cactus or an earthworm could meet their criteria and so they went back into pairs to think again.

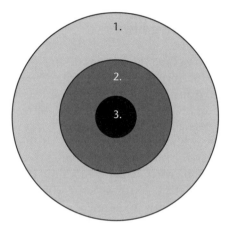

Figure 6.3 Target

This sort of exercise in evaluative thinking could be applied to any subject area for learners of any age. 'What is it that makes a good pet?' could be replaced by 'What is it that makes a good poem?' or 'What is it that makes a good scientific hypothesis?'.

Using the target-setting strategy for clarifying content thinking is obviously useful. However, the teachers I interviewed about this strategy[iii] were most excited by the potential of this technique to help them involve children and young people in their own assessment. It could be used to negotiate with students what the success criteria should be for a given task such as: explain the water-cycle, write a short poem about rain, draw a snowflake or make a light switch – every classroom task can be given explicit shared success criteria. Assessment can then be done in many ways: by individuals assessing their own work, groups assessing each other's work or the whole class assessing the work of each group.

Thinking about criteria in advance of the activity really helps students to focus on what is most essential. Once again, as with all the strategies, this is a great stimulus for productive talk in which key thinking words are introduced and practised in motivating dialogues. For example, there is great scope for discussing appropriateness of criteria. When teachers set criteria, they are often tempted to choose standards they know everyone in the class can achieve because they don't want to discourage anyone. So when they set criteria for a marketing poster they may say: 'Make sure it has a title, an illustration, some slogans and a paragraph of explanation'. This is obviously far too vague and general – rather like the children's criteria for pets mentioned earlier. Children could make some pretty bad posters that met all the criteria. At the same time, there is a danger of setting quality criteria too high, and far outside the abilities of some pupils.

An alternative is to discuss ideal criteria for a poster and then, using the target strategy, encourage pupils to set their own criteria for success according to their own perceptions of their abilities. And there is always room for discussion about whether the criteria they set themselves were too easy or difficult.

Living Graphs or Fortune Lines

Living Graphs or Fortune Lines map the feelings of one or more of the characters in a story along a timeline. So while reading Little Red Riding Hood, for example, the teacher encourages her children to think about how the wolf is feeling at the beginning of the story when he is hungry and alone, then how he might feel as he meets Red Riding Hood, and then when he eats up Granny and so on.

An important aspect of the approach, as with all the thinking strategies, is to question children's first answers thus prompting more reflection. For example, 'Would the wolf really have been happy when he saw Red Riding Hood or only when he learnt about where she was going?' or 'Are you always sad when you're frightened?'.

One teacher used this technique to follow the feelings of both Little Red Riding Hood and the wolf over time. In groups, the children can be given key events from the story and asked to mark them on a timeline (the horizontal axis of the graph). Then the group has to decide how the wolf felt and how Little Red Riding Hood felt on a scale

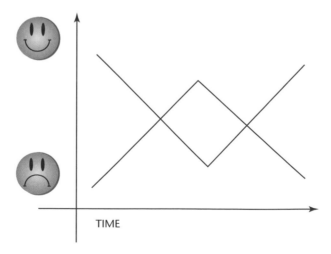

Figure 6.4 Fortune Line

of 'miserable' to 'ecstatic' which can be defined on an interactive whiteboard using a smiley face and a sad face (see Figure 6.4). This normally produces two different lines on the graph that might cross at key points. For example, when the wolf says 'all the better to eat you with' he probably feels elated at the prospect while Little Red Riding Hood feels terrified, but when the woodcutter turns up the tables are reversed. The teacher who reported this said that the activity not only supported great discussion but helped her young pupils access the whole idea of graphs, which are important to mathematics and science, through their empathy with characters in a story they loved.

In a religious education class, a living graph of the last days of Jesus, comparing his feelings with those of Judas, stimulated much reflection. How did Judas feel as he betrayed Jesus with a kiss and how did Jesus feel at that point? As with all the strategies for infusing the teaching of thinking into the curriculum the aim is to provide a support and framework for fruitful discussion – not only in adding to curriculum knowledge but also in providing an opportunity to use and master key concepts and ways of using language to question and to reflect.

Normally graphs are only used for numbers but really they are a very general tool for supporting generalization and abstraction. Using this technique children learn to link specific, concrete incidents to an abstract representation.

Diamond Ranking

Ranking Lines and Diamond Ranking (where the first and last items are few but the middle items can be many) are simple but sometimes surprisingly effective tools to support thinking. They require pupils to consider what makes some things more important than others and to reflect on degrees of and criteria for importance. They may also lead pupils into discussions of appropriateness as in the example below.

One teacher reported that her most exciting lesson was a variation on ranking. It happened when her class took over the teaching and organized themselves to decide on the best adjective to describe the lead character in a book that they had been reading. The first stage was to generate a list of alternatives and to rank them. Each of the most popular terms was given a position on a line on the floor, and pupils had to move to stand in the position given for the adjective that they chose. Debate ensued and pupils moved between positions. The book was *The Tulip Touch* by Anne Fine and the word they started with was 'malevolent' but they ended with 'evil'. However, I illustrate the basic idea of the exercise with a different possible word set (see Figure 6.5). Whatever the words, dictionaries have to be consulted and arguments given. The conclusion itself was not as important as the discussion about particular meanings of descriptive concepts and the principles of appropriateness based on evidence and interpretation.

Diamond Ranking works for anything that requires judgement and prioritizing. It could be introduced with a fun example like choosing a present for a friend. But it can be applied to stimulate thought and discussion in any area of the curriculum. The idea is that there are five levels of importance and the most important thing goes in the top slot and the least in the bottom slot and everything in between somewhere in the middle three rows. This is best used to support group work in threes and could be

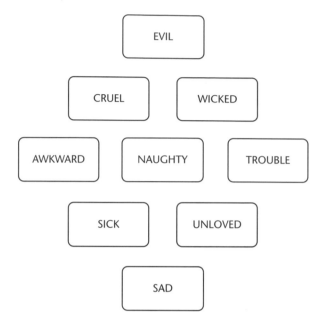

Figure 6.5   Diamond Ranking

used with a whole class debriefing on a whiteboard. The plenary is a chance to explore different judgements and values.

Mysteries

In the strategy Mysteries small pieces of information are given out which relate to an overarching question.

This is a popular strategy that can be used at any age and for every subject. Pupils are usually asked one big open question, often about the cause of an event, such as 'Who was responsible for the Great Fire of London?'. Different levels of 'clues' on the information cards help children to piece together details about the baker, the layout of the city, the lack of a fire brigade or the unwillingness of the aldermen to agree to the creation of firebreaks as the fire raged, to promote discussion about the fire in order to develop an understanding of cause in history. Data is provided on small slips of paper that pupils, collaborating together, can move around their table as they develop, shape and evaluate ideas. The data, when seen as a whole, usually has a storyline, some characters, important topic-related subject knowledge and, possibly, some red herrings.

Pupils start by sorting the bits of information into those that they think are relevant and those that are not. They have to interpret and make links to put the cards in categories (feedforward), check and refine their sorted groups (feedback) and form a view of the cause of the disaster. It is most important that pupils are allowed to define their own categories and change them as their thinking develops. They will often come up with categories at first like 'causes' and 'not causes'. After reflection and rearrangement they may develop into categories such as: 'most likely causes', 'least likely causes', 'causes with supporting evidence', 'causes supported by hearsay' and so on.

The pupils are engaged in thinking activities such as sorting, classifying, sequencing and making links between the single data items (the parts) and their theory (the whole). They are making inferences and using evidence as they give reasons for their ideas. The activity encourages the use of concepts such as *class*, *category*, *consequence* and *evidence*. Pupils are asking questions, posing and defining problems and testing and improving ideas. They are often creative in generating theories about the causes of the event under scrutiny and they have to evaluate the theories of their own group and of others.

There is much scope here for rich learning discussions during the debriefing sessions. Students can rehearse questions about causation and discuss feedforward and feedback strategies they used. Dispositions such as adventurousness, carefulness, dialogue, collaboration, reflectiveness and persistence, are all exercised by Mysteries. Students learn, through dialogue and persistence, that their first thoughts on a subject may not always be the best.

In Felton First School, Barbara Pratt and Gwen Curry demonstrated that Mystery investigations do not require writing and reading and so can be used effectively with very young children. One powerful Mystery they developed involved filling a suitcase with an assortment of items they claimed had been found by the road. The children's task was to work out who the owners of the case were, where they were going and what they were doing. Although Barbara and Gwen put related things in the case like a map showing beaches marked with an X, a towel and flippers, they also included 'odd' items to stimulate children's imaginations such as a mechanical mouse or a Batman mask.

The teachers had taught their children to use the verbal forms 'I agree because' and 'I disagree because'. The combination of this preparation for talk and the lost suitcase Mystery activity led to a great deal of quality reasoning about claims and evidence. Other Mysteries developed at the school, like the one mentioned above about what caused the Great Fire of London, produce reasoning about causation and part and whole relationships.

A number of these kinds of strategies have been developed. They are all teaching techniques but share common features. These powerful pedagogical strategies[iv] are difficult to define precisely. They tend to exhibit some (or all) of the following characteristics:

1   **They are re-usable structures**. Once a class has been introduced to the kind of activity they can quickly undertake another task. Having done Odd-One-Out with pictures of animals and with types of materials in science, the class went on to do similar activities in mathematics with numbers and shapes, in English with characters from traditional tales, in geography with pictures of landscapes. The teacher needs to spend very little time explaining what to do, so the lesson focuses very quickly on the content being learned.

2   **The tasks do not have a single correct solution**. They are open-ended and encourage a variety of working methods and reasoning. With Odd-One-Out any item in the collection can be the odd one out so long as there is a valid and reasoned case. Similarly with a Fortune Line a teacher might present ten short episodes from an act in *Romeo and Juliet*. For each episode, students are asked to plot the emotion (despair and sadness or happiness and ecstasy) of a character or characters on a vertical scale, thus charting their intertwining and changing emotions through the act as events unfold (on the horizontal axis). The teacher's choice of extracts from the play for the class to sequence and analyse helps to frame the discussion. There is no single correct answer to this task, it calls for interpretation. The strategy therefore helps to legitimize the opinions of all pupils, as all that is required is a reason. Their answers or solutions are justified either by their reasoning or by their preference for a certain way of handling or processing information. However, it is important to appreciate that whilst there may not be a single right answer there are probably better answers which require explicit justification. Good thinking is the goal of the activity with explicit reasoning respected.

3   **They encourage talk, articulation and dialogue**. As the tasks often contain productive ambiguity, they present information in a way that demands interpretation, clarification, connecting, hypothesizing and evaluating, which are the kinds of talk that are prized for their role in helping pupils jointly construct understanding. Working in and as groups is an essential ingredient of the use of the strategies, as is whole class discussion to compare solutions and reasons from different groups.

4   **They are flexible** and can be used with different ages and in different curriculum subjects. Odd-One-Out can be used from infants to postgraduate settings to identify and sharpen conceptual understanding of how things are classified and categorized.

5   **They represent a manageable unit of change**. Odd-One-Out can be introduced as a short activity in a single lesson lasting no more than five minutes or so. Banned takes longer and requires more preparation and management. A Mystery would normally need a full lesson for the group work and the debriefing afterwards. All of the strategies are understandable as teaching tasks, and therefore easier to get started with than, say, developing a more open style of questioning or more pupil talk as developmental objectives. The structuring of the task provides a scaffold for the teacher to get started. The accessible nature of the tasks, presented as games, puzzles or challenges, also makes them easier for the pupils to understand what they have to do.

6   **They encourage teacher creativity and enquiry**. The purpose of the strategies is to promote active exploration of the benefits and limitations of the technique so that teachers can add it to their repertoire of activities. Odd-One-Out can be a simple diagnostic activity, perhaps at the beginning or end of a unit of work, to provide the teacher with information about how fluent learners are with particular ideas and concepts. It can also be part of a more systematic enquiry into the kinds of responses and understanding that

learners show. For example, some teachers have found that high attaining pupils tend to be more adventurous and creative in their Odd-One-Out choices and reasons. Less successful pupils tend to play it safe and stick to reasons they are confident with, and so are less likely to try out new vocabulary or ideas they have recently been taught.

7   **The strategies change the nature of subject knowledge and its relationship with the learner**. The National Curriculum in England and Wales has, some might argue, encouraged a view of subjects as bodies of knowledge to be learned. By contrast, these kinds of strategies aim to get the learner to draw on what they know as the task begins, juxtaposing the new with the known. Subject knowledge is therefore presented as a stimulus for further reasoning. To elaborate on one of the examples above, identifying the emotional state of Romeo requires the use of knowledge of the play and Romeo's character, as well as a more personal understanding of the situation either from experience or vicarious knowledge through watching films. Talking about this in a group combines curriculum content knowledge with personal experience in an activity of understanding something new.

When these strategies are used as a stimulus for dialogue and for thinking then it is also possible to reflect on learning, perhaps through a class debriefing discussion or by looking back and reviewing learning when the strategy is used the next time. Because the strategies and techniques can be used in a variety of subject settings they can help in the development of an awareness of and a language for describing learning, or learning to learn (I say more about this in Chapter 8).

The following quotations come from teachers' reflective diaries written when they were working with the strategies in recent years. They confirm the importance that pupils' responses have to teachers. Some of these quotes give a strong sense of the impact the students' response is having on plans for future practice and beliefs.

> The pupils were staggered at the fact that they had more than one chance to come up with an answer.... They were even liberated.... I just had to harness this opportunity. (History)

Commentary: It is the pupils' response to the openness and ambiguity of the task that captures the teacher's attention here. As pupils realize that they can reason their way to alternative solutions they are described as 'liberated'. Significantly the teacher signals the need for a response in practice to 'harness this opportunity'.

> Pupils gave answers in vocabulary that peers understood – the fundamental difference is the freedom to discuss.... The children found the lessons entertaining and engaging. (Maths)

Commentary: The impetus here for the teacher is the vocabulary that pupils develop to construct their own understanding in discussion. The teacher appears to be encouraged by the fact that pupils are motivated and engaged.

> As one walked around the room one could hear the various reasons behind ideas as well as other members of the group questioning each other's responses and thinking. (RE)

Commentary: What has captured the teacher's attention here is the quality of the dialogue between pupils. It is interesting too that the teacher has begun to eavesdrop on discussions rather than to intrude or intervene. This practice places one in a much stronger position for debriefing as one can call on groups to contribute their reasoning to a whole class forum. It indicates to the students a level of respect for their contributions.

> One of the most notable and pleasing features . . . was the number of pupils' that commented upon the fact that they were encouraged to listen and value other people's opinions. Some of the pupils commented that this had made them change their own way of thinking . . . writing was detailed, emotional and analytical. (History)

Commentary: This account shows linkage between developing pupils' interaction, a feature of more dialogical exchanges, leading to some changes in learners' thinking and leading ultimately to more skilful writing.

> Demotivated pupils miraculously transformed into pupils showing superb skills in explaining, listening to one another, efficient team work and using higher order skills, such as classification and selection of material. It has shown me that all pupils, whatever their levels of ability or interest, can become involved and enthused as a whole class and subsequently providing a classroom environment in which good, active learning is taking place. (Geography)

Commentary: The teacher's enthusiasm is clearly related to the pupils' engagement. There is a strong suggestion that the transformation of pupils' responses that this teacher experienced is leading to a change of beliefs which will interact with their pedagogical knowledge.

> For the first time at . . . , pupils questioned me about an issue. This is something that just doesn't happen here. (There is) a tradition of what pupils are told is right, and they must learn this, not necessarily understand. . . . It really promotes pupil confidence . . . pupils were no longer asking me 'Is this right?'. (They are) learning to have confidence in their answers, and learning to have their own opinions. (Geography)

Commentary: A change in the pattern of talk or discourse has struck home for this teacher. Teachers normally dominate and control whole class talk through asking questions, but here pupils are reversing the flow, which in the teacher's judgement is promoting their self-confidence and perhaps their self-concept.

> The response was certainly positive and they felt that it helped them listen carefully to others. One pupil said that it was more tiring than a normal lesson because he felt that the responsibility rested on him to make sure that he did not let his group down. (MFL)

Commentary: Listening is a key requirement of language learning. Not only has the teacher seen an improvement but she has had her eyes opened to one avenue to encourage this, namely collective responsibility.

Teaching thinking and the curriculum

All of the teaching strategies described in this chapter provide opportunities for pupils to try out different approaches to problems, evaluate their strategies and internalize appropriate questions and concepts. The National Curriculum thinking skills are referred to as follows:[v]

Children learn how to:

1 **investigate**, asking relevant questions, identifying problems, analysing and judging the value of information and ideas, questioning assumptions. They plan systematically using time and resources effectively, anticipating, taking and managing risks

2 **create and develop**, using their imagination to explore possibilities and generate ideas. They try out innovative alternatives, looking for patterns, recognising differences and making generalisations, predicting outcomes and making reasoned decisions

3 **communicate**, interacting with different audiences in a variety of ways using a range of media

4 **evaluate**, developing criteria for judging work and suggesting refinements and improvements.

All of these skills are supported by the teaching thinking strategies. 'Setting targets' supports evaluation, 'Mysteries' support creative generation of hypotheses as well as enquiry skills, the 'Odd-One-Out' is perhaps obviously a context for recognizing differences and all of them support communication.

Steve Williams argues that these strategies work to teach thinking by providing an opportunity to use key concept words as tools to think with. All the strategies provide a structure within which key thinking words, strategies and tools can be introduced and then practised. Through this the pupils can learn how to engage in reasoning with others, how to pursue a shared enquiry, how to ask relevant and responsive questions, how to use tools like ranking tables and graphs, and how to use key thinking words.

Each of the strategies also focuses on some concept words more than others. Table 6.1 developed by Steve Williams, shows some of these relations.

These and similar words are used across every area of the curriculum and every area of life as tools to help us think about problems and pursue shared enquiries. To think well pupils need to be given the motivation and opportunity to master these words and ways of using them to support thinking together with others.

This focus on mastering conceptual tools provided in the language fits the socio-cultural approach to understanding teaching thinking that I described in the first chapter as the tool-use metaphor. I contrasted this to the metaphor of dialogue. However,

Table 6.1 Strategies with associated concept words

Odd-One-Out	similar, different, same, significant, category, quality, respect, conclusion, alternative, opinion, possible
Mysteries	cause, effect, category, important, relation, quality, respect, argument, symptom, opinion, conclusion, possible, alternative, proof, evidence, question, idea, sort, special
Diamond Ranking	important, significant, part, whole, alternative, degree, measure, order, organisation, sort, opinion, decision, similar, same, special
Living Graphs	measure, part, whole, important, significant, order, sort, organisation, example, special, change
Setting Targets	measure, necessary, degree, purpose, relation, type, comparison, example.

this contrast should not be seen as a simple dichotomy. Learning how to use key words is part of learning to think, but the use of these words is learnt in the context of dialogues that motivate their use. The sort of distinctions that concept words enable children to make expand and enrich dialogic space. Seeing concept words as thinking tools implies a vision of them from the outside. The danger of this, discussed in Chapter 5, is seeing concepts as a closed system in which all meanings are defined. In reality, in the flow of thinking, concept words are more like voices or, better, like lights, that illuminate new aspects of the shared landscape of a dialogue and even seem to bring new features, fissures, peaks and dimensions into being.

The powerful pedagogical strategies that I have described in this chapter work to promote thinking within the curriculum by opening up spaces for dialogue. These dialogues are not completely open, they are content related, they offer a chance to practise using important concepts, but nonetheless they work to teach thinking by drawing children into a dialogic space. They are useful when the topic being taught is so complex that it helps the children if you approach it through an activity that breaks down that complexity, making it more easy to grasp. For instance, the idea of looking at the emotional development of characters in stories is not an easy topic to approach in a primary classroom. A living graph makes this complex idea much more accessible.

Another value of the strategies is in scaffolding the development of thinking skills. For example, any advanced thinking will use the concepts of similarity and difference developed through the Odd One Out exercise. But, of course, once children have grasped these and can use them it is not necessary to teach everything through Odd One Out type activities as this might limit the development of more complex dialogues in which multiple concepts are integrated.

As I discussed at the end of Chapter 4, a dialogic relation is possible with a subject area as well as with another person. In fact, if you want to be creative in a subject, and really understand it from within, it is essential to establish that dialogic relation that I described in Chapter 4 through the idea of reversibility or the chiasm. Powerful pedagogical strategies provide opportunities for understanding the curriculum in this way. They provide opportunities to draw children into dialogues within content areas. These are bounded 'fields of dialogue' teaching specific content in terms of the kinds of dialogues that you can have in a field. This involves positions that can be taken up but also the important concepts and the kinds of arguments that can be made.

Chapter Summary

This chapter presents several simple but powerful strategies to teach almost any subject in a way that will, at the same time, support dialogue within the curriculum. This approach is not being advocated as a total alternative to the more generic dialogic education approaches put forward in the rest of the book, approaches like Philosophy for Children, Thinking Together and Building Learning Power. It is more a kind of scaffolding for injecting dialogic spaces into curriculum areas where they did not exist before. The main benefits of this approach are in breaking down the teaching of complex conceptual content into an easily graspable activity and in practising some of the component skills of dialogic thinking.

7 Thinking and creativity with ICT

Chapter Overview

ICT is going to be one of the core subjects of the new primary curriculum in the UK along with literacy and numeracy. This probably reflects the concern of the government to make sure education prepares children for the economy of the future. The current transition from an economy based on the production of material goods to one based more on knowledge has led governments everywhere to emphasize the importance of teaching children how to use new information and communications technology. Along with creativity and thinking skills, new media literacy is one of the core knowledge-age skills required for thriving in the knowledge age. In this chapter I describe the distinctive way in which ICT can support teaching for understanding and teaching for thinking and creativity.

Skills for the knowledge age

In the small villages near where I live in Devon many specialist shops have closed over the years but one local butcher is thriving. This butcher, Dave Haggett, has found a way to offer his traditional butchering skills on the Internet. He advertises a hog roast service as well as his award winning pies and sausages. Dave's story illustrates how the Internet has made it easier for some to sell or swap traditional goods. Online auction sites like 'eBay' keep many small producers in business. Incidentally, they also provide a good opportunity for children, working with parents and teachers, to acquire business sense and numeracy skills.

While the Internet is good for helping to distribute traditional goods its main strength still lies in making the exchange of new knowledge goods easier. Blogs and global social networking sites like 'facebook' and 'YouTube' have expanded enormously in the last few years. While the first wave of Internet development was mainly putting up information from one to many, this second wave, often called Web2.0, is more about participation, with many people putting up their own material, as well as commenting and engaging with others. These sites make it much easier than it ever has been for anyone at all to offer something from their own experience to everyone else in the world. There have been many success stories where previously unknown individuals have become famous and made a career for themselves. For example, one 13-year-old schoolgirl, Tavi, wrote a blog on fashion that got so much attention that she was taken up as resident blogger by a top fashion magazine and now spends her time flying to top fashion events. In an interview she described herself as 'a tiny dork' whose passion for fashion was not understood by her friends and teachers at school so she made a home for herself on the internet.[i] Tavi's case illustrates the absurdity of the still often repeated accusation that spending evenings at home with a computer screen is 'anti-social'. There may be issues about the balance between face-to-face and electronically-mediated communication but most contemporary ICT use is the opposite of 'anti-social', it is about as social as it is possible to get.

In dictionaries education is often described as preserving a culture by transmitting the accumulated experience of the past to new generations. The rapid pace of change challenges this rather backward looking idea. Mobile phones, the Web, even call centres, did not exist when many of the people now working in industries based around these new technologies were at school. How well did their education prepare them for their future lives? Those entering formal education now will almost certainly experience a future that is very different from the world of today. How can we best help them to thrive in that future? Children like Tavi are already seizing the opportunities that ICT offers to participate and engage. It seems that, in most cases, children and young people who are engaging with the knowledge-age economy are doing so despite their schools rather than with the help of their schools. It is still very common to find access to the Internet restricted and mobile phones banned in schools that treat new technology as a threat rather than as an opportunity.

The big idea behind the term 'knowledge age' is that we are moving from an economy based on the manufacture, distribution and consumption of physical goods, things like cars and fridges, to one based on knowledge. Knowledge covers many things from software for making new cars work, Dave's traditional sausage recipes, the expertise of fashion commentators like Tavi and even education itself. The kinds of jobs people do when they leave school have changed over the last thirty years and are still changing. Local factories used to be the major employers for school leavers. Now manufacturing goods only accounts for about 3 million jobs in the UK, just over one-tenth of the total. Hi-tech knowledge-based industries have been the main source of new jobs. These industries are various but are defined by the fact that they invest more in research and development and in 'human capital' (i.e. in education) than they do in physical things like machinery. The so-called 'creative industries', such as writing books and making films, designing video games, producing TV shows and recording new music etc., also make up a fast growing area of the economy, a sector that earned £9 billion in exports in 2008 and now employs nearly 2 million people.[ii] On current trends it will not be long before this booming creative sector overtakes manufacturing as a source of employment.

All the signs indicate that we are living through a revolutionary transformation in the economy and that the growth of electronic communications, especially the Internet, lies behind this revolution. In the industrial age only a few people, the factory owners, had goods to sell. What excites me about the knowledge age is that we now all

have something unique to sell: our unique experience of the world according to us.[iii]
The Internet makes it possible for each individual to offer what it is that they do best
and that makes them special to the rest of the world. I have mentioned Dave Haggett's
traditional recipes for sausages and schoolgirl Tavi's flare for fashion, but there are many
more original approaches to making the Internet provide a living. The main limit to
this expanding new economy often seems to be our imagination.

Bernie Trilling, head of Oracle Education (Oracle is one of the biggest IT companies
in the world, second only to Microsoft), describes the skills we need for the knowledge
age as the Seven Cs (see Table 7.1):

Table 7.1 Skills for the knowledge age as the Seven Cs[iv]

Seven Cs	Component skills
Critical thinking and doing	Problem Solving, Research, Analysis, Project Management, etc.
Creativity	New Knowledge Creation, 'Best Fit' Design Solutions, Artful Storytelling, etc.
Collaboration	Co-operation, Compromise, Consensus, Community-building, etc.
Cross-cultural understanding	Across Diverse Ethnic, Knowledge and Organisational Cultures
Communication	Crafting Messages and Using Media Effectively
Computing	Effective Use of Electronic Information and Knowledge Tools
Career and learning self-reliance	Managing Change, Lifelong Learning and Career Redefinition

While this is just one list it is reasonably representative of the range of lists articulating
the skills needed to survive and thrive in the knowledge age.[v] With their focus on
creative and critical thinking as well as on learning to learn, knowledge-age skills are
clearly similar to the general thinking, creativity and learning skills and dispositions
that I write about in the rest of this book. However, the list also includes ICT skills like
media literacy and the effective use of new technology to manage knowledge and to
communicate. ICT is not a separate subject but needs to be integrated into creativity,
communication, thinking and learning across the curriculum and across the whole
of life. Schooling needs to help children use ICT to engage effectively in the global
dialogues that will shape their future. And in a very real sense, which I will expand on
later, using ICT to engage in global dialogues is precisely what it means to teach for
thinking, creativity and learning to learn.

What is ICT?

ICT in education used to be referred to as just plain IT, standing for information technology, and it still is in many parts of the world. The C for communications was added
in the UK in 1997.[vi] This looks like an advance but it raises a conceptual issue. Does
this idea that we can simply combine information technology and communication

technology really work? There are two concepts involved that used to be thought of as quite distinct: the concept of a tool and the concept of a medium of communication.

To use a tool you need three things: A) a subject with an intention, e.g. a man with a hammer and a plan, B) the tool itself, e.g. the hammer with some nails, and C) an object, e.g. the fence to be fixed by the man with the hammer and the plan.

Media, such as language or music, are not like this at all. Sometimes language or music can be used as a tool just to get something done. A musical ringtone of the beginning of Beethoven's Fifth Symphony could act as a prompt to you to pick up your phone. But really language and music are much more than tools just as Beethoven's Fifth is much more than a ringtone.

Asking 'What is the purpose of language?' or 'What is the purpose of music?' leads us to realize that there is an important distinction to be made between tools that have a purpose outside of themselves, like hammers or screwdrivers, and media that are often simply ends in themselves. In a sense we dwell inside language and music and construct ourselves within them: they should be understood as a medium for being, not as tools to get stuff done. The same is true of new media, digital TV, video games, multimedia websites and so on. These are not tools for a purpose we have determined in advance but they are ends in themselves.

Is the same perhaps true of ICT? Rather than thinking of communications technology as a tool system for getting stuff done perhaps we should think of it more as a medium, opening spaces for dialogue and for playful expression?

People say that the Internet has been expanding exponentially since its inception in the last decade of the twentieth century. But expanding is a spatial concept, what does it mean in this context? Into what space exactly is the Internet exploding so rapidly? Clearly the expansion of the Internet is not only about how many more kilometres of fibre-optic cable are used or the number of computer servers linked into the system but is much more centrally about the websites, blogs, messages and virtual communities through which people interact together. In sum the Internet opens up and gives an almost concrete form to the idea of 'dialogic space'. And, as we have argued in the other chapters of this book, entering into dialogic space is the key to learning thinking and creativity.

ICT and education for creativity

In Chapter 3 I described how the concept of creativity has two poles, imaginative play (creativity 1) on the one hand and fashioning a socially valued product (creativity 2) on the other hand. ICT bridges these two poles because it allows children, quickly and easily, to produce high quality finished products in a range of media. The provisional and infinitely correctable nature of ICT encourages creativity and risk taking, while the finished quality of ICT enables a take-home product every child can be proud of.

Learning to write creatively provides an illustration of what ICT can do. Drafting is the key to good creative writing but when a 6-year-old has struggled for many minutes to laboriously write a few words on a bit of paper with a pencil they do not want to go back, rub words out, and try again. They may get disheartened and learn to hate writing if you keep telling them to do this. This is a problem because redrafting is the key to good creative writing, shifting from creativity 1 to creativity 2. It is much easier for children to redraft and so to be creative using a word-processing program, where they can cut and paste and copy and delete as much as they like.

Before he could write his own stories my son loved to use a program called 'Huggley's Sleepover'[vii] which created amusingly silly stories for him, around items that he had to choose. The stories were displayed in clear text and read out by the program moving from word to word. They were a key part of Huggley monster's sleep-over party. He always laughed when he heard them read out and he felt proud of them. Later he moved on to writing his own multimedia books preferring to type rather than to write with a pencil because it looked better and was easier to correct. Not only did ICT use effectively scaffold his introduction to literacy but it made it intrinsically creative throughout. And incidentally, in case you are wondering about handwriting, that does not seem to be a problem with my son or the many other children who now learn to type at the same time as they learn to use a pencil.

In Chapter 4 I argued that the origin of creativity lies in dialogues. Dialogues always stimulate unpredictable responses. And they have a sort of infinite generator of new ideas at their heart whereby my response to your response to my response can go anywhere at all within a few steps. In fact the only thing that you can be certain of in a dialogue is that the other person will not understand what you say in exactly the same way that you understand it. The greater the difference between people held together in the creative tension of a dialogue, the greater the potential for creativity. In enabling dialogues across distance and differences ICT can facilitate creative dialogues. Collaboration between children and artists, writers or fictional characters in 'non-residence' through email and video conferences illustrates this.

Junior children in Robin Hood School in Birmingham used video conferencing facilities to establish contact with artist Nick Eastwood, to look at his work, to ask him questions and to receive feedback from him on their own work created in response to the experience. In another example, the Bristol Internet Project, children in schools in two different communities in the city collaborated with each other on making visual images over time and distance. They used digital cameras and 'Paint' programs to construct images of themselves which were attached to email messages to their 'key pals' in the other school, asking questions such as 'Who am I?'. Artists in each school worked with the children to interpret, respond to and manipulate the images received before sending them back with their developed ideas.[viii]

The key characteristics of ICT that support creativity are that it is:

- provisional, so everything can be changed with little cost.
- interactive, it responds to you.
- collaborative, easy to share and work together.
- of finished quality, delivering something to be proud of at the end.
- multimodal: 'I love the picture; can you say the same thing in music?'.
- automatic, it can do all the boring stuff required to realize a brilliant idea.[ix]

These features lead to an intrinsic relation between creativity and ICT. Once it took long years to be able to turn ideas into working models. Now, with the right software package, primary age children can quickly engage in designing and running fairground rides, designing new houses and cars and even designing their own new bodies (avatars) in virtual reality worlds. As well as a dialogic space ICT provides an in-between space, a space bridging the two sides of creativity: the side of unbounded imagination and the side of fashioning high quality products.

Computers as mindtools

I have written about ICT and creativity so far but what about ICT and more rigorous reasoning such as critical problem solving? Here the mathematics educator, Seymour Papert, has had a major influence. His ideas lie behind the fact that LOGO, a logic-based programming language, is currently used in all UK primary schools. LOGO is the language used to program roamers, robots that can be made to travel around the floor of the classroom, and turtles, their counterparts that travel around a computer screen. In 1980 in an influential book called 'Mindstorms: Children, computers and powerful ideas'[ix], Papert criticized the use of computers as teaching machines, and argued in favour of using computers as a tool for general intellectual development. His approach, he wrote, was about allowing the kids to program the computers, not letting the computers program the kids. It is not a coincidence that Lego's range of programmable robot kits is also called *Mindstorms*, Papert was invited in by Lego to help them design it (I wish I had that job. If any Lego executives are reading this, please contact me).

Early in his career Papert researched the development of mathematical reason with the Swiss psychologist Jean Piaget who is often referred to as 'the father of constructivism' in modern education. For constructivists learning occurs when children construct theories and models to explain experience. In his introduction to *Mindstorms*, Papert offers an example from his own life to illustrate his view of the potential role of computers as a constructivist learning tool. He describes how a fascination with mechanical gears as a young child gave him a concrete way to understand and visualize all kinds of mathematical functions from multiplication to differentiation. Playing with gears, he claims, laid the foundation for his later career as a mathematician. Just like the gear set he had as a child, he believes that computers can be used to give complex abstract ideas a concrete form that can be manipulated by children. But since computers are massively more flexible than gear sets their power lies in offering children a huge range of resources with which to develop their minds.

An abstraction like the force of gravity that is hard to teach in a science classroom is easier to understand in a simulated environment where the child's in-world avatar can try out the experience of jumping on planets of different sizes. In a similar way, what Papert called 'mathematical microworlds', like the LOGO environment where it is possible to program turtles to move around a screen, enable learners to engage with abstract ideas as if these were concrete things. This approach to using ICT to teach thinking has been called the use of computers as 'Mindtools'.[xi] The idea is not that computers will directly teach thinking but that, through working with computers, the student will be encouraged to think logically and by doing so will acquire internal cognitive tools for their own later use in other contexts.

Programming in LOGO is a good example of the use of computers as a mindtool in this sense. Some of the general thinking skills that have been claimed to result from programming include:

- learning problem solving, problem finding, and problem management strategies such as breaking a problem into parts or relating it to a previously solved problem.
- learning how to plan and to undertake the kind of diagnostic thinking involved in debugging.
- practising formal reasoning and representation such as thinking of all possible combinations, and constructing mathematical models.
- valuing positive cognitive styles such as precision.
- emphasizing a reflective approach over an impulsive approach.
- reinforcing attributes such as persistence and enthusiasm for meaningful academic engagement.[xii]

This all sounds quite plausible but an important proviso has been left off the list. Children who learn to program probably do have to learn to use at least some of these skills and attitudes. However, it does not follow that skills they learn in the context of programming will transfer to be useful to them in other situations. This seemed to be assumed by Papert but is the sort of question that is worth testing through research.

Since the publication of *Mindstorms* in 1981 the logic based programming language LOGO, promoted by Papert, has been widely used and evaluated in schools around the world. There have been many evaluations and there is no evidence that its use has led to any dramatic increase in abstract thinking or general thinking ability. Research suggests that working with LOGO alone does not in itself automatically produce any general thinking skills that transfer to uses in other contexts. The evidence is rather that this kind of transfer only occurs when teachers plan activities and experiences that help to make it happen.[xiii] The combination of elements required for this includes whole class dialogues, in which the teacher shares thinking aims and a thinking vocabulary, and small group dialogues in which children have a chance to articulate and so take ownership of new general thinking strategies. In other words the research evidence points once again to the importance of engaging children in dialogue as the source of transferable thinking skills.

An example of an ICT lesson with LOGO

The Thinking Together approach works well to bring a dialogic element to almost any computer task that can be done in groups. Working with teachers and research colleagues I used the combination of Thinking Together and LOGO for programming a robotic roamer with a class of 6-year-old children. The aim of this activity was to teach the transferable skill of writing a clear set of instructions. The difficulty of writing clear instructions, the sort of instructions that could be followed by anyone anywhere, lies in abstracting from experience only the essential elements that are required to achieve a task. Robots are excellent partners for this training exercise in abstract thinking because they really do know nothing other than what the children tell them. The lesson began with a whole class exercise in which the link between giving clear instructions and programming a robot was made through giving volunteer children wearing blindfolds instructions as to how to move around the room. The children were asked to do nothing other than what they were told to, so unless they were told to stop they would keep walking until they hit the wall. This dramatizes in an amusing way the need for absolutely explicit and context-free instructions.

In preparation, the ground rules for Exploratory Talk and Thinking Together vocabulary were rehearsed by the teacher who also modelled the use of 'because' to give reasons in response to a challenge or disagreement. Then the children were asked to work in groups, applying the ground rules to devise a program or set of instructions that would send the roamer around a specific route on a large floor mat. Discussion helped the groups to achieve this task, challenging and correcting each other's ideas of what to put in the program. Each set of instructions was tested by another group using a toy car on the mat before using the roamer. The small group work developing and testing programs gave children the opportunity to articulate and understand the central idea of generating explicit instructions that were both sufficient and precise. In the groups' discussions the general thinking skills embodied in Exploratory Talk were applied to develop aspects of thinking appropriate to computer programming. In a follow-up activity the same general principles were applied to writing clear directions for visiting different shops using a map of a town. In the closing plenary the teacher emphasized the general principles involved in writing a clear set of instructions and so made a bridge between the two contexts of programming the roamer and writing directions for others to follow using a map.

Using games to teach strategic thinking

There is a lot of writing now about using video-games in education. There is no evidence that games, or any other software for that matter, can teach thinking skills on their own. However, games can be used as a resource to help teach thinking when made part of teaching and learning dialogues. In this combination games are motivating and are a powerful way of teaching strategic 'If...then' type thinking. For example, funded by the Nuffield Foundation, I investigated combining teaching Exploratory Talk with using mathematical strategy games. One of the games we used was similar to *Connect Four*,[xiv] the aim of the game being to place four counters in a line on a grid on the computer screen before your opponent does so. Counters are positioned by typing in co-ordinates. We[xv] focused in on the point where children shifted from acting procedurally to developing a strategy for winning. We found that some groups would literally repeat the moves which enabled them to win for the first time but the computer often changed its moves so that the children then lost. To win every time they needed to shift from procedural to strategic thinking. In some examples they spontaneously developed new terms to describe the strategies that they found, for example, the phrase 'two-way-trick' to describe a situation where they could win with either of two moves and so could not be blocked from winning by the computer. Reconstructing the conditions that led to the emergence of strategic thinking we found that the role of the teacher in pointing out strategies to the children was important, although the teacher's suggestions were not always taken up. Also important was the role of dialogue between children. Simply asking 'Where should we go?' or 'Why do you think we should put it there?' led to reflection and the emergence of winning strategies.

The findings of this research project with SMILE mathematics software suggest strongly that once children have been inducted into effective dialogue for thinking and reflecting together (Exploratory Talk), then playing strategy games *against the computer*, where a small group of children work together to try to beat the machine, can be a highly motivating context for shared reasoning and problem solving. This context reinforces the use of Exploratory Talk because the children can see that it works; as one young girl put it: 'Talking about our moves really helps us win against the computer'.

The most effective pedagogy for using strategy games can be summed up in the following steps:

1) introduce the game and reinforce 'our rules for talking' (the Exploratory Talk ground rules established earlier).
2) get the children working around the computers in groups of three trying to beat the computer at the strategy game (I know lots of computer rooms do not support this – rearrange them!).
3) intervene to reinforce the rules for talk by modelling them, (e.g. 'Have you asked Josh what he thinks? What are your reasons? Do you all agree?').
4) have a plenary in which the rules for talk are revisited, the children describe any good or bad talking experiences, but the focus is on each group explaining strategies that worked to the whole class and discussing why they worked.

This approach could be applied to any strategy game including the many popular online and stand-alone computer games that require planning, decision making and strategic thinking such as *Age of Empires* or *Sim City*.

However, for teaching thinking it is not enough just to play games. By playing games children might learn how to win the game but they will not necessarily understand how they won. For developing strategic thinking of a kind that might transfer beyond the specific game context to other tasks it is important that they have to talk to others in order to explain the strategies that they used.

From IRF to IDRF: Dialogues within the curriculum

In the new primary curriculum in England and Wales ICT is to be integrated across the curriculum. Combining Exploratory Talk and work in small groups with computers is an excellent way to do this. Computers can be very motivating but one of the first rules for teaching thinking through dialogue is to break the fascination with the screen to get children to sit back and reflect. Children closely engaged in interaction with the interface enjoy clicking buttons and observing the almost instant response, in a way that can make any discussion difficult. The idea is to open up a dialogic space. This then becomes a dialogic space within the curriculum generating reflection, thought and understanding, guided towards a curriculum topic.

As I mentioned in Chapter 5, linguists have labelled one of the most common language patterns found in classrooms, and almost only in classrooms, as the IRF exchange structure. IRF stands for Initiation, usually a question by the teacher, Response, by a student, and Feedback by the teacher. For example, a classic IRF could be:

> Teacher: How many sides does a hexagon have?
>
> Pupil: Seven?
>
> Teacher: [3 second pause] Does anyone else know?

This three-part exchange structure allows the teacher to keep control of the direction of the interaction with students. The student's input is always framed by the teacher's prompts and evaluations. As a result the IRF exchange structure has been criticized by those that claim that it controls students too much and prevents them from thinking for themselves and asking their own questions.

With group work at the computer, after some preparation in the ground rules of dialogue, the educational exchange can be different. The computer program may take the initiative and pose a question (I), it may also insist on a response from a limited range of options (R) and finally, it may evaluate those responses either explicitly or implicitly through the choice of follow-up questions (F). However, when dealing with computers, a pair or groups of users have a new option. That option is to sit back from the computer screen and discuss their response together.

Discussion between the 'Initiation' and the 'Response' introduces a new kind of educational exchange which can be called I*D*RF to signify: Initiation, *Dialogue*, Response, Follow-up.[xvi]

I*D*RF exchanges supported by computers, mobile devices or whiteboards combine two very different kinds of interaction. The 'IRF' part refers to the user-computer interaction and the '*D*' to the spoken pupil-pupil dialogue. I*D*RF also combines two very different educational genres. Taking the IRF sequence alone, users appear passive and the computer appears to be in control. This may be taken to correspond to what is sometimes, usually in a pejorative sense, called a transmission model of teaching and learning. In dialogue mode, on the other hand, users actively consider their options using the information offered by the computer in the knowledge that the conclusions of the discussion will later be tested out upon the computer. In this moment of the educational exchange the interaction with the computer acquires the more passive role of a 'learning environment'. The '*D*' part of the I*D*RF exchange therefore corresponds to active engaged learning.

Through the IRF framework the computer can stimulate and direct the talk of the children in order to meet the goals of a predefined curriculum. In the discussion moment children construct their own meanings. In Chapter 5 I gave a good example of this where the mechanical 'Talking Bug' opens up a dialogic space in a science simulation forcing children to think together more about how sound waves travel. I*D*RF exchanges with ICT provide a way of teaching any and every content through dialogue while also teaching thinking and creativity.

The Forum Design

The way in which the *D* moment of dialogic reflection could expand out of the IRF framework to take over the educational activity is clearly illustrated by another type of interface designed for reflection and debriefing at the end of an interactive story or game. I called this 'The Forum' and it consisted simply of a decision which the users had to make taking into account the views of all the characters in the story (see Figure 7.1). In the first 'Forum' the group working with citizenship software I created called *Kate's Choice* are asked to decide if they made Kate 'do the right thing': whether she told that her friend Robert had stolen chocolates to any of the characters who put pressure on her, or if she did not tell and allowed herself to be falsely accused. The structure of this Forum screen is shown in Figure 7.1 with all the characters' heads around a central space where text boxes appear with their views when they are clicked on. It is very crude and simple as I made it myself some time ago. It could easily be implemented on an inter-active whiteboard perhaps using photos of pictures by the children. Note that there is

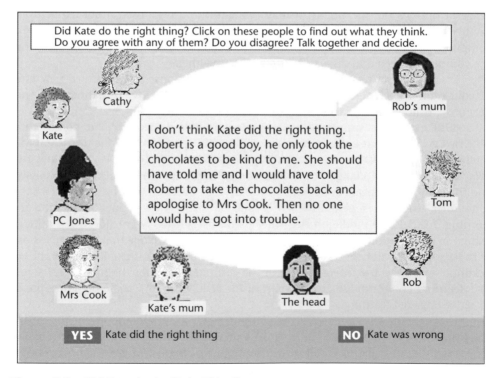

Figure 7.1   Did Kate do the Right Thing?

a single question 'initiation' or 'prompt' at the top of the screen: 'Did Kate do the Right Thing?'. And only two buttons to choose from at the bottom: YES or NO. This is again an IRF interface design with the main twist being that before they make their decision they are asked to engage in dialogue with the points of view of all the characters in the story.

With some groups the combination of teaching Exploratory Talk with this software design produced a great deal of serious dialogue and deliberation before the final decision was made. Here is the dialogue transcript of one group of 9-year-olds:

Transcript extract

[Computer text initiation:	'Did Kate do the right thing? Click on these people to find out what they think. Do you agree with any of them? Do you disagree? Talk together and decide.']
Kath:	[Clicks on Rob's mum and then reads the screen text shown in Figure 7.1]
	'I don't think Kate did the right thing. Robert is a good boy. He only took the chocolates to be kind to me.'
Alan:	No, I don't agree.
Kath:	I don't agree with that –
Alan:	That's just wrong.
Kath:	Robert's mum should be on Mrs Cook's side really.
Alan:	Yeah. She should be more strict.
John:	Next round. Kate's mother. [Clicks on Kate's mum]
Alan:	OK [reads from screen] 'Kate did the right thing to tell. She should not lie to me or hide things from me. I am her mother.'
Kath:	All right John – you go first this time.
John:	I think that's all right actually, because if you don't tell her, and her mother finds out she's going to get really done because she ain't told her mum.
Kath:	Yeah, then Kate's mum will go round to Rob's mum's house and say 'You did this and you did that and your son is a bad influence to my daughter.'

Alan:	'Cos he stole.
Kath:	But that's wrong as well. I know Kate <u>should</u> have told her mum – and that's what she did, but if Kate didn't tell her mum, then Rob's mum would sort of fall out with Kate's mum because I think Rob's mum and Kate's mum are friends so I think Kate's mum is right. I agree with Kate's mum.
Alan:	Yes. I think about Kate's mum – and it's also good for Kate, because she'll have a really guilty conscience and she'll feel really upset inside. And she'll –
Kath:	And it will all start to bubble up inside her and she'll just have to tell somebody.
Alan:	And Rob, I think if he doesn't get told now what's right and what's wrong, when he gets older he's going to get into a lot more trouble than just a box of chocolates.
Kath:	Yes – in older life there's no second chances. He'd better start learning.

This dialogue fulfils the stated aim of the citizenship curriculum to encourage children to discuss moral issues together. The activity provides them with an opportunity to take charge. They appear to relish the chance to criticize the positions of adults such as Rob's mum and to assert their own moral opinions.

The strength of this design is that it inducts learners into dialogue in a specific domain in a way that is focused on a particular issue but not bounded in any way. In the 'Talking Bug' illustration given in Chapter 5 the children are encouraged to discuss sound insulation in order to be led to construct the right answer for themselves which is that cork insulates best because of its low density. However, in this citizenship example the aim is not to induct the children into a right understanding or a correct voice. The aim is rather to induct the children into this field of debate in a way that encourages them to understand the issues and find their own voice as a position within this field. Of course a pro-social ethical approach is being taught here but the ethics are democratic ethics, about empathizing with others and listening respectfully to all points of view before making decisions together. In the talk the learners called upon their experience and practised voices drawn from a range of contexts, for example the idea of a guilty conscience making someone 'upset inside' expressed by Alan or that 'in older life there are no second chances' expressed by Kath. This illustrates how the opening of a dialogic space allows many voices to enter in and inter-animate each other in a way which creatively opens up new possibilities.

The very simple forum design described above is particularly suited to the interactive potential of computers. It does not need to be limited to artificially constructed debates of the kind described, but, in combination with use of the World Wide Web, it can be used to induct learners into real debates between different perspectives on any and every issue. Web-quests, for example, can be structured not as a 'finding out the truth' type of exercise but more as an 'exploring the space of debate' type of exercise. This is as true of 'hard' science questions like the potential impact of global warming or the various interpretations of quantum theory as it is of more obviously philosophical questions like 'Is stealing always wrong?' or 'What should be the aim of education?'. An excellent example of the educational power of the forum design combined with web multimedia can be seen at: http://www.playthenewsgame.com/. Here young people can role play being real participants in current events and so learn to understand comlex issues from multiple perspectives.

Understanding teaching thinking with ICT

Experience of what works and what does not in the teaching of thinking supports a dialogic account of how we can best teach thinking. This can be applied to the role of ICT in teaching thinking. In fact ICT is crucial to a dialogic account of teaching thinking once we go beyond looking only at the individual child in a face-to-face classroom. The quality of thinking is not found in individuals it is found in dialogues. Some of these dialogues are face-to-face but increasingly ICT is allowing for new dialogues across distances and differences where dialogue was not possible before. Those who resist or resent the role of ICT in education and argue for the primacy of face-to-face learning sometimes seem to miss the bigger picture. It is not possible to teach the world to think better together without ICT being involved. And if we do not combine education and ICT effectively to teach the world to think better together then we are condemning our children to the same perpetual warfare that characterizes almost the whole of our history.

I understand dialogic education with ICT as about opening, widening, deepening and resourcing dialogic space. Below I take each of these terms in turn to outline a coherent overall approach.

1 Opening dialogic spaces: The importance of preparation for talk

There are ways of using ICT in education which close down dialogic space and ways which open this up. Tutorial software with a question and a multiple answer response often closes down dialogue where the aim becomes remembering the right answer (nothing wrong with drilling in the right context of course, but it does not teach thinking). Interestingly though, I have found that exactly the same sort of questions and tasks given to a group who have been encouraged to talk together through the Thinking Together programme, will open up dialogic spaces within the curriculum. Once children have been empowered to talk together even simple questions with yes/no responses can stimulate long sessions of thoughtful dialogue. Another example of the importance of preparation and task design is that simulations that encourage fast and furious engagement will close down dialogue, whereas the same interfaces with a prompt for talking that interrupts the action, open up dialogic spaces (see the 'Talking Bug' example in

Chapter 5). A singular affordance of new media technologies is the possibility of supporting new dialogic spaces anywhere and everywhere, from interactive blogs under exhibits in museums to text exchanges between pupils in different classrooms. But the technological support alone does not make a dialogic space. One of the key findings from my research on collaborative learning around computers in classrooms is that, for effective shared thinking, it is not enough just to place people in groups but they need to be prepared for working together in groups beforehand.[xvii] Applying discourse ground rules such as asking open questions and listening with respect to others opens up a creative dialogic space around almost any stimulus.

The same principle that effective shared thinking needs to be positively taught emerges from reviews of collaborative learning in online environments.[xviii]

Interactive Whiteboards transforming the classroom into a single dialogic space

Research on the best ways of using the new technology of Interactive Whiteboards (IWBs) is still in its infancy. It is interesting that some of the larger government funded studies now seem to be finding IWBs useful for introducing dialogic pedagogy. The size of the screens and their capacity to support interaction and direct manipulation lend support to creating an almost tangible dialogic space in the classrooms. Sara Hennessy of Cambridge leads one such large research project on IWBs. She describes lessons with the teacher sitting at the back of the class encouraging students to come up to the screen to annotate existing materials, scrawling their reactions to pictures, adding notes to text, or arranging items in order of importance or connectedness. The IWB saves every screen so initial thoughts can be returned to at the end of the lesson for reflection on how opinions have changed, or at the end of a series of lessons.[xix]

Many of the dialogic teaching suggestions in this book could be enhanced by making use of the larger dialogic space supported by IWBs. For example, teaching science with concept cartoons could be enhanced by asking children to put up pictures of themselves on the IWB and write their thoughts about a science issue in speech bubbles. These thoughts could then be returned to and reflected on after an experiment or a series of experiments that gives them deeper insight into the issue.

Another study into IWBs led by Neil Mercer reports that these classroom tools enable children to easily:

- access material which is relevant to their task, and move easily back and forward through it according to their needs.
- annotate that material to take account of their developing discussion.
- remove and modify what they have written to take account of each other's views and their changing shared ideas.
- ensure that all members of the group can see what is being discussed, and members' contributions as annotations to the material.
- offer advice to each other about their annotations or other treatment of the material (e.g. the selection of specific slides, or searches for relevant information).

The researchers on this project found the idea of opening and working within a dialogic space very useful for their analysis of the extra potential that the IWB brought to the classroom, writing that the IWB 'seemed to help keep them within the dialogic space, and to avoid being distracted'.[xx]

2 Widening dialogic spaces

Students broaden their understanding of a space of debate when they are better acquainted with the range of positions that are possible; they deepen it when they are able to explore a single bit of the argument and its assumptions and implications. Broadening or expanding means roughly increasing the degree of difference between perspectives in a dialogue while maintaining the creative relationship. Broadening can be done through the use of the Internet to engage in real dialogues about global issues. A good example of pedagogical use of the potential of the Internet to support dialogue across difference can be seen in the educational development site: http://www.throughothereyes.org.uk/ where different groups of young people around the world provide their own accounts of what is important in their lives.

Inter Faith Dialogue by Email: Illustrating widening

InterFaith dialogue provides a very interesting model for dialogic education. This is because, in contrast to most accounts of argumentation in education, it is not about changing minds, it is all about deepening understanding. In the E-Bridges project primary children in schools in Leicester were twinned with children in schools in East Sussex. Each child was paired with 'an email friend of a contrasting religious and/or cultural background from the partner school' and they had timetabled exchanges weekly throughout the school year as well as some residential visits.

The aim was partly to counter fractures along racial, cultural and religious grounds in Leicester. It was located within the citizenship curriculum goal of 'understanding and appreciating cultural and religious difference, thinking about the lives of other people with different values and customs, seeing things from others' points of view'. But the timetabled sessions took place within RE because the focus was on religious difference. There were four stages of dialogue:

1) Introduction: In this stage the email partners got to know each other as people with particular hobbies, likes and dislikes, friends and family. Questions asked include, 'What do you like doing in your spare time? What are you especially good at?'
2) Sharing experiences: The children compared and contrasted their experiences of celebrations, special places and practices. The kind of questions explored at this stage were, 'Are there any times of year that are particularly special to you? Why are they special? How do you celebrate them?'

3) Ethical debates: These included discussions around such questions as, 'Is it ever all right to kill a living creature? Do you think that human beings should eat meat? Could it ever be a good thing to use violence? If you had one message that you could tell the whole of humankind what would it be?'

4) Questions of faith: Questions have included: 'What do you think happens to you when you die? Do you think someone who has been bad will go to hell? Do you believe in angels? If not, why not, and if so, what are they for?'

In face-to-face class or group discussions there is the danger of a few children dominating the group. In email dialogue, all the children have an equal chance to make their views known; all are required to think in order to respond. Though it may be difficult to match the quickfire pace of spoken dialogue in electronic communication, it does provide the benefit (particularly to younger dialogue partners) of thinking time. As a child initiates an exchange, she has time to think carefully about how she is going to express her views or frame her question. Children receiving emails have opportunities to think carefully about what has been said and what their responses might be before making their contributions to the discussions.

The following checklist of key questions helped pupils frame their responses to emails:

- Have I considered the needs of my partner?
- Have I offered my own views on the topics being discussed?
- Have I given reasons to back up my views?
- Will my partner understand the words I am using?
- Have I given my partner a question or problem to think about?

For some of them the dialogue flowed naturally and easily, others needed support to move the dialogue forward. Teachers encouraged them with phrases that helped to organize their thinking. Some of these are set out below:

Clarification
When you said ... what did you mean?
I didn't understand what you meant by ...
Could you please explain ...
What do you mean by ...?

Extension
What do you think about ...?
If ... would you think the same?
Does that mean you also think ...?
Is that the same as ...?
What if ...?
Do you think it would be the same if ...?
I would like to know your ideas about ...

Affirmation
I like the idea...
My ideas about...are very similar to yours
I agree with you when you say...
I think...too

Disagreement
I agree with you about...but I don't think...
You said...but I think...
Don't you think...?
But if...then...
I can't agree with...because...
If you say...then that means...[xxi]

Very similar projects have been conducted successfully between schools researching questions together in other areas of the curriculum. Not only do such projects widen dialogue about a topic they teach the essential knowledge age skill of how to collaborate in a team online to achieve a project together.

3 Deepening dialogic space

Deepening refers to increasing the degree of reflection on assumptions and grounds. With the right pedagogy the broadening potential of Internet dialogues also becomes a deepening as students are led to reflect on the assumptions that they carry with them into dialogues. Talk in face-to-face dialogues exists only momentarily and only for those immediately present. Technologies that support drawing and writing can thus be thought of as a way of deepening dialogues, by turning transitory talk and thoughts into external objects that are available to learners for discussion and shared reflection.[xxii] Computer documents can offer a kind of halfway stage between the evanescence of talk and the permanence of written texts. Harry McMahon and Bill O'Neill, the originators of *Bubble Dialogue* software, use the term 'slow-throwness' to refer to the way that their tool can externalize the thoughts and feelings of the participants and also support reflection and the possibility of returning and retrospectively changing dialogues. The first version was used to promote inter-cultural dialogue between Catholics and Protestants in Northern Ireland.

At the heart of *Bubble Dialogue* is the simple idea of combining pictures with speech and thought bubbles. The pictures are easy to load into the software and can represent dialogues in any situation. In addition to the bubbles there is a facility to review the dialogue created so far and to change it and also, of course, the option to print it out. With Harry McMahon's support I designed and had developed a new multimedia version of *Bubble Dialogue*, which I call *Bubble Dialogue II*, in which there is also an option to record speech so that children do not need to type but can talk instead.[xxiii]

To give one example of this, we used *Bubble Dialogue* in a special school for children with emotional and behavioural difficulties. Such children can find it particularly difficult to articulate their own thoughts and feelings and to appreciate others' thoughts and feelings. Teachers at the school believed that collaborative use of the software has great potential value. An example of such dialogue is provided in the bubble dialogues reproduced in Figure 7.2 and extract 1 below. This was created by Charlene and Rory, both aged 10 years, and both excluded from their previous schools because of behavioural difficulties. They are discussing a bubble dialogue scenario about a personal conflict involving characters called 'Joe' and 'Greg'. In the story Greg was using his new skateboard in the playground when Joe, a bigger boy, grabbed it from him.

In the first exchanges both characters 'square up' for a physical fight. However, the next set of think bubbles that Charlene and Rory produced (see extract 1) indicate that while both parties are prepared to fight over the skateboard, 'asking nicely' or apologizing would diffuse the situation.

Transcript extract 1 (bubble dialogue): Joe and Greg

Joe thinks: He'll just have to ask nicely.

Joe says: I'll kick your head in you fat brat head.

Greg says: Yeah come on then, I'm not scared of you – if I'm a big fat brat head what does that make you, you peabrain.

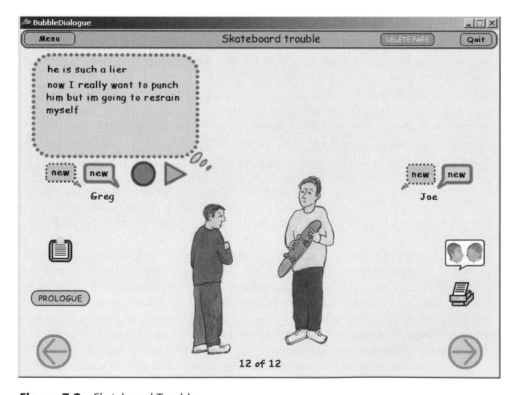

Figure 7.2 Skateboard Trouble

Greg thinks: I'm not scared of him, all he's got to do is give me my skateboard back and apologize to me, if he doesn't I'm going to break his big fat ugly bogied up nose.

Charlene and Rory's story goes on to have Joe give Greg the skateboard back. When Greg insists on an apology Joe denies having taken the board and says that Greg should say sorry for threatening to punch his lights out when he was only playing. Eventually they both manage to apologize in a guarded way and agree to be friends. Their thoughts remain angry but their words are conciliatory.

The expert teachers of children with emotional and behavioural difficulties are convinced that these kinds of conversations can equip children like Charlene and Rory with inner resources to draw on in real life situations. Through using the *Bubble Dialogue* program they rehearsed a way to talk themselves out of a fight that at first seemed inevitable.

Teaching thinking is more typically seen in terms of learning how to solve reasoning tests. Here we can see the same dialogic mechanism increasing reflection and awareness not to solve an IQ type test but to solve a real-life problem and increase emotional intelligence.

ICT and creative dialogue between media

Meaning can be explored using a variety of media. According to the dialogic across difference perspective I have outlined above, dialogues are not simply an exchange of words. They consist of a relationship between voices or perspectives motivating a flow of meaning. This flow of meaning is focused and articulated by signs and communications technologies but is not reducible to those signs or technologies. Exploring the dialogue between meanings in different modes has the potential to broaden dialogues, by giving access to new kinds of perspectives and to deepen dialogues, by encouraging one mode to reflect on another. For example, asking students to reflect on musical representations of different arguments can give access to the emotions that are often implicit behind neutral seeming words in texts and so both broaden and deepen the dialogic space. This can be illustrated through a recent project in a school in the UK where the use of ICT was central. This was a creative workshop combining together music composition, dance movement and artwork using light to produce a response to an initial poem entitled 'Light Shifts'. The multimodal result, presented in PowerPoint, is a powerful expression of multimedia dialogue effectively evoking that 'dialogic space' between and around different media that enables meaning to transgress and to transfer. Figure 7.3 gives an edited version still combining light and text but to this you have to add in imagination, movement, music, and voice.

Resourcing dialogues: openers and maps

As well as opening, widening and deepening the space of dialogue, in conjunction with new ways of teaching, new communications technologies also offer new ways of resourcing dialogues. By the term 'resourcing' I mean simply that they provide tools

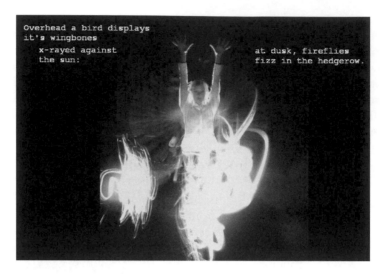

Figure 7.3 Lightshifts[xxiv]

and structures. One example of this is a series of experiments using 'dialogue games' to help induct young people into productive discussions. Another is the use of dynamic concept mapping.

Normally online dialogue is presented in the form of a list of utterances like a play script. This is different from normal face-to-face dialogue because the spatial presentation means that lots of people can 'take the floor' and speak at once and the dialogue takes a written form that can be preserved and reflected upon. The sort of problem that can arise is that by the time you have replied to one utterance the argument has moved on.

One support for this was developed by Andrew Ravenscroft and provides an interface that helps people follow the argument and to 'scaffold' the argument by providing a list of openers coupled with a list of possible responses. For example the opener might be 'I think that ....' and the response might be 'I disagree because ...'. The current system is called InterLoc and it has mainly been used with university students but the potential for use of this kind of approach in schools is obvious. The evidence suggests that it helps students overcome their reluctance to challenge and be more robust in their argumentation.

Another way of supporting online dialogues is with dynamic concept maps. The maps are made up of message boxes of different shapes and colours representing different types of contribution and links between them which can also be given a meaning. The end result is not a list of messages in temporal order, but a spatial pattern. This supports reflection since the children discuss the maps they have produced all together afterwards.

The use of space is a resource shaping the awareness. While a list may naturally suggest linear development towards a single conclusion, arranging shapes in the space of a map allows children to explore different ways of looking at an issue. Evidence suggests that this co-presence of multiple points of view in one space stimulates creativity in dialogues.[xxv]

The shapes are also a resource. A system called Digalo comes pre-packaged with argument shapes based on the Toulmin scheme described in Chapter 5. This means that for each shape children can decide if it is a claim or evidence or perhaps a challenge. This is obviously useful for teaching argumentation. But the shapes are very flexible and I adapted this to use it with Edward de Bono's Six Hats; each 'shape' had a different colour, black for the negatives, white for logic, green for creativity etc. I asked students to use all the different shapes when thinking about an issue. They reported that this helped them to gain insights that would not have been possible without this resource.

The need for teaching and learning dialogues

This chapter has summarized some of the findings of recent research on ICT and thinking skills.[xxvi] One principle to emerge from this review is that using computer-based technology on its own does not produce transferable thinking skills. The success of any ICT activity crucially depends on how it is framed by teachers. Learners need to know what the thinking skills are that they are learning and these need to be explicitly modelled, drawn out and reapplied in different contexts.

Another principle to emerge is that collaborative learning improves the effectiveness of most activities. Computer mindtools such as programming languages also all appear to be enhanced when used in pairs or groups especially when students are taught to explicitly articulate their strategies as they work together. Throughout this book I advocate the Thinking Together approach to ICT use, a collaborative approach in which children are aware of the crucial importance of their discussion. Group work becomes meaningful as children understand how to do better together than they could alone. They also understand that by working thoughtfully with others, they are learning how to think more clearly in situations when they must work alone.

The approach to using ICT to teach thinking that I am advocating can be summarized in four points each of which assumes the crucial importance of teachers:

- The class undertakes explicit teaching and learning of dialogue skills which promote thinking.
- Computers are used to bridge learning through dialogue into curriculum areas using the IDRF exchanges structure.
- Introductions and closing plenaries are used to stress aims for talk and for thinking as well as to review progress within the curriculum.
- Teacher intervention in group work is used to model good shared thinking.

Thinking and the World Wide Web

Thinking occurs in dialogues but these are not just local face-to-face dialogues, there is also dialogue with ideas, dialogue with the past and dialogue with the future. It has always been true that thinking is a collective enterprise with no boundaries. Our words carry traces of the thought of our ancestors, as well as influences from every part of the globe, and there is no telling where they will end up. But new communications technology, especially the Internet, is beginning to give a heightened tangibility to the vision of universal dialogue that has always been implicit in thinking. Michael Bakhtin, for example, a scholar of ancient Greek texts exiled to a remote part of the Soviet Union, dreamt of what he called 'Great Time', a kind of dialogic space in which all ideas would be understood because all voices from every culture would be able to speak together. Many of the texts he loved are now available in the original Greek and in multiple translations on the World Wide Web. So are ancient texts in Sanskrit, and Chinese and Hebrew. Wikipedia and other sites provide spaces for dialogue about those texts. Blogs and sites like 'YouTube' and Oxfam's 'oneworld' provide opportunities for people from every culture to put their point of view in video form as well as in pictures and writing. The Web is now the first place to find out about new ideas or movements whether these arise in Tokyo, Isfahan or in a remote part of Mexico. This Web 2.0 support for dialogues and collaborative learning across the world has so far been mainly for adults. However, Web 2.0 social networking sites are now becoming available for primary children that expressly address safety issues while helping children engage in collaborative learning (for example: http://www.boaki.com/). For me at least this direction is not towards chaos but towards the expansion of collective consciousness.

For this positive vision of more universal and global thinking to be realized it is not enough for the resources and voices to be out there on the Web. It is essential that children are given the basic skills and dispositions needed to engage constructively with those resources and voices. Learning to think with the World Wide Web gives an almost concrete form to the old idea that learning to think is learning to participate in the thinking of a collective mind which has no boundaries.

Chapter Summary

There seems to be no evidence that children reliably learn general thinking skills just by working with computers, including the programming languages and 'mindtools' that have been promoted as a way of learning to think. However, there does appear to be good evidence that some ICT activities can be used to teach general thinking skills when used as a resource for teaching and learning dialogues. Talking to others while working at the computer encourages the articulation of strategies and so increases the likelihood of learning skills that can be transferred to new situations. The teacher has a role in making the thinking aims of activities explicit, modelling good thinking strategies and designing learning activities so that skills learnt in one context are applied in new contexts. But perhaps a more important role of the teacher is in preparing children to learn for themselves from the rich resources of the internet. This is about learning how to be safe, how to critically evaluate content and how to learn collaboratively with others. Teaching thinking with ICT can be understood as expanding the mind by opening, deepening and widening dialogic spaces. ICT makes it possible to open spaces of dialogue in any subject area. These dialogic spaces can be deepened using tools that support critical reflection, simulations for example, that make it possible to explore consequences. ICT can also widen these dialogic spaces by bringing in new perspectives, either role-playing these in controlled computer games or interacting with real other people through the Web.

8 Mind expanding

Chapter Overview

In this concluding chapter I draw together the main themes of the book and locate them in a vision of education. The evidence all points to the fact that it is possible to teach children in a way that leads to more thoughtfulness and more creativity. The kind of teaching that does this best works by drawing children from narrow identities out into relationships with other people and other perspectives that are different and challenging. The quality of thinking is not found in following rules but in the quality of responses to the challenges that others pose and that life poses. Education for thinking is also education for responsibility; both for taking responsibility and for being able to respond with wisdom when challenged. Teaching for thinking and creativity is not just about helping prepare young people to be happy and successful in their futures, it is also about participating in shaping that future and making the world just that little bit better than it might have been otherwise.

I began this book examining the argument that it is not possible to teach thinking. The main argument is that:

1) thinking is always about something,
2) and since how you think well depends on the something that you are thinking about,
3) it follows that there is no 'thinking in general' that can be taught.

The examples of successful ways of teaching for thinking and creativity illustrated throughout this book show that this argument cannot be right. Successful educational practice tells us about the nature of good thinking. For example, attempts to teach thinking in the abstract through teaching formal rules of thinking have largely died out because they have not been successful. The most successful approaches stress the quality of relationships and draw children into real dialogues with teachers, with each other and even with puppets. These approaches seem to work not by teaching a discrete set of thinking facts and procedures but mostly by developing good thinking dispositions.

The evidence from educational practice points to thinking being dialogic. The dispositions that make for good thinkers are related to becoming a more dialogic kind of person: that means being open to the voices of others, happy questioning everything and comfortable in a situation of uncertainty. The best context for developing this disposition for being more dialogic is by drawing children into real dialogues about things that mean something for them. Again the evidence suggests that teaching thinking through engagement in dialogue in the classroom is not as difficult as you might think. Stressing a few simple ground rules can transform dialogues and lead to high quality thinking: ground rules such as listening carefully, building on what others say, exploring all possible alternatives, responding to challenges with reflection and perseverance, and giving reasons and asking for reasons. The most difficult bit for parents and teachers is perhaps the modelling. To be able to model good thinking it is essential to practise good thinking.

Skill at dialogue implies openness to others and a willingness to respond but also a questioning attitude, both questioning to make sure that you have heard what has been said and questioning to find out if it really makes sense. Developing a disposition to be open yet questioning towards others in a dialogue will lead children also to be open yet questioning in the face of new ideas. To understand something is to listen to it and rephrase it in your own words in a way that makes sense to you in the context of your world. Teaching for insight and understanding, as opposed to teaching for parrot-like repetition, is always therefore dialogic teaching.

Learning how to learn: an example of how to teach for thinking and creativity

Many of the key points about teaching for thinking and creativity that emerge from this book as a whole can be illustrated by a successful approach to teaching 'learning how to learn' devised and implemented by Guy Claxton and colleagues. The Building Learning Power[i] programme focuses on developing dispositions that will support thinking, creativity and learning to learn. Some of its components are found in the other approaches I have explored in the book but it also has new elements.

This approach involves the way teachers talk to children, organize their classrooms and design activities, as well as the way that they teach. It calls for teachers to be constantly discussing how to develop learning power with students and encouraging children to use the language of learning. It is based around the idea of four key learning dispositions, which Claxton calls the four Rs:

- **Resilience**: 'being ready, willing and able to lock on to learning'. Being able to stick with difficulty and cope with feelings such as fear and frustration.
- **Resourcefulness**: 'being ready, willing and able to learn in different ways'. Having a variety of learning strategies and knowing when to use them.
- **Reflection**: 'being ready, willing and able to become more strategic about learning'. Getting to know our own strengths and weaknesses.
- **Reciprocity**: 'being ready, willing and able to learn alone and with others'.

These four Rs are further explained by Claxton as follows:

> Developing learning power means working on four aspects of students learning. The first task is to help them become more resilient: able to lock on to learning and to resist distractions either from outside or within. The second is helping them become more resourceful: able to draw on a wide range of learning methods and strategies as appropriate. The third is building the ability to be reflective: to think profitably about learning and themselves as learners. And the fourth task is to make them capable of being reciprocal: making use of relationships in the most productive, enjoyable and responsible way.[ii]

In looking at other approaches like Thinking Together, Dialogic Education, Philosophy for Children, Accountable Talk and Thinking at the Edge we have already explored many of the aspects of teaching for thinking and creativity covered within these 4Rs. However, the one that is not really covered in the other programmes we have looked at so far is, Claxton writes, the most important one: *Resilience*.

Claxton breaks *Resilience* down into four components:

- Absorption, flow: the pleasure of being rapt in learning.
- Managing distractions: recognizing and reducing interruptions.
- Noticing: really sensing what's out there.
- Perseverance: 'stickability'; tolerating the feelings of learning.

He argues that teaching in a way that will develop these dispositions involves many aspects of classroom life including things like:

- the way teachers explicitly talk to students about the process of learning.
- the visual images, prompts and records on the classroom walls.
- the kinds of questions children are expected to ask, and the kinds of follow-up they are expected to make to such questions.
- the way teachers respond to students when they are experiencing difficulty or confusion.

But the key quote here is 'above all else, perhaps, is the way that teachers present themselves as learners – what kind of model or example they offer, for instance when things are not going according to plan, or when a question arises that they had not anticipated' (Claxton 2002).

This emphasizes the way in which learning is embedded in relationships and reiterates the point I made right at the beginning of the book. Teaching for thinking, creativity and learning is hard because it requires that the teacher also has to think seriously about things, respond creatively to events and love to learn.

An interesting example of the impact of applying the Building Learning Power (BLP) approach comes from Solihull where the Local Authority worked closely with Guy Claxton. Most headteachers began by nominating a member of staff to get trained in the approach and act as a coach for the school. An evaluation of the approach by local headteacher Marilyn Phipps notes that particularly effective practice was seen in a group of schools who collaborated as part of a Learning Network. This involved combining INSET days and staff meetings, using Advisory support and visits to schools within the network to share ideas and good practice. Marilyn explained that: 'This extended way of working offered greater potential for developing creative approaches to BLP and was also more supportive for staff who were feeling fragile or even plain scared!'.

In pupil interviews, especially in primary schools, the most frequently quoted benefit of BLP was the improvement in the ability of children to persevere. Classroom environments also changed, for example resources became more accessible and displays were more likely to support learning rather than only to celebrate learning. Children were observed using the new classroom learning resources to support maths learning and in interviews they confirmed this. One KS1 child said, for example: 'If I'm stuck I look at the BLP board and I see persevering and I keep trying.'

Marilyn concludes her report with some words from the children:

'BLP has helped me recognise that I can do things.'
'I used to cry when I couldn't do my work. I don't any more.'

In one school involved in this project, the headteacher Jackie Cannings wrote that:

Using BLP as a whole school initiative has enabled a common learning vocabulary to develop in school. This has meant that the ethos encourages the learning vocabulary to be central to our work. In mathematics it has been exciting to see children persevering during problem solving and able to talk about this in 'BLP' speak as well as mathematical talk. Children are absorbed in their learning experiences in the classroom which they can articulate and again the focus on language developed enables staff and children to have common understanding.[iii]

I have described Building Learning Power and quoted from a report of its implementation because I think it is a good demonstration of how it is eminently possible to teach for thinking. Teaching thinking is not about teaching a set of facts and procedures: it is about teaching dispositions that shape responses within relationships. These relationships are not only with other people, including parents and teachers, but they are also with more nebulous things like areas of knowledge or new ideas. The evaluation from Solihull suggests that we can improve children's ability to think and to learn if we isolate the key dispositions and habits of mind needed for thinking and learning and break down the factors that shape people's dispositions and habits within classroom life. In keeping with the dialogic thesis of this book, the one thing that makes the most difference is the model of how to be a human being that is offered to children by the adults they interact with. If as a society, as a school system and as parents or teachers we really want to promote better thinking then we have to care about thinking ourselves.

The importance of words

I quoted above a headteacher claiming that it was really useful to have a shared vocabulary for talking about thinking and learning. This is a common finding from successful teaching thinking programmes. If every teacher and every pupil can point to issues with thinking and learning like perseverance, being brave (in coming up with new ideas that might be wrong) or finding evidence, then that shared vocabulary will help raise awareness of these issues and of thinking and learning in the school in general.

Some have even argued that learning to think is essentially about learning to use thinking words.[iv] In every area there are key concept words to learn. But as well as these there are many relationship words which help children to think within areas and between areas. Words like general and specific, cause and effect or part and whole.

Going beyond words

That using words is important to thinking is obviously true but it is also true that thinking goes beyond words. The research into children's talk while solving reasoning test problems that I described in Chapter 2 can help us to understand this relationship. Words did not help Tara solve the problem. In fact at first she could not put her vision of the solution into words at all. But she kept trying and came up with a phrase, 'taking the circle out', that communicated it to the others. Putting things into words like this made a relationship in the patterns visible which had not been visible before. The phrase 'taking the circle out' became part of the shared ground that helped the group solve some of the next problems in the series, problems characterized by similar relationships like 'taking the little square out'. Successful talk for solving reasoning test problems had a lot more words and phrases like this than the unsuccessful talk. Groups who learnt to solve the tests better shifted from pointing at the paper saying simple things like 'Look, cos . . . ', to pointing at shared words, saying more elaborate things like: 'Look, cos they are taking the circle out there and here the cross is turning from outside to inside the triangle'.

What we can see when we look at research on children thinking together in classrooms is how words embody understandings so that they can be shared. But each new solution of a problem is creative. To solve a problem thought takes off beyond the level of understanding embodied by existing words to go further into a kind of wordless vision. Then the understanding returns to clothe itself in words, taking up existing words in new ways to make new phrases or even sometimes inventing new words to fit a new vision like the creation of the word 'fantabuloso' described by Neil Mercer and reported in Chapter 3. Understanding can be spread by these new words and phrases but only when people inhabit them and use them to see with. In a sense these key words support thinking and understanding by acting like lights with which to see things rather than, as has been said, by serving as 'tools' or as 'building bricks'. In the example I gave in Chapter 2, Perry repeats Tara's phrase, 'taking the circle out' but he does so with excitement and animation while looking at the puzzle because the phrase gives him access to a vision. It helps him to see it in a new way making a relationship visible that was not visible to him before.

Words and insight

Words are important but insight and understanding occur in a space beyond words and then need to be clothed in words. How can we characterize the space beyond words where insights occur? A clue is given in the way in which open questions and challenges often stimulate new thoughts. When Perry asks Tara, 'What do you mean?' she is stimulated to see the problem in a new way and change her mind. When the teacher Mark Prentice asks Alex, 'Is it really real?' (in the example of thinking given in Chapter 3) Alex is projected into deeper reflection on his experience which leads to deeper insight. In sum I think that insights occur in spaces of reflection that are opened up between voices in dialogue.

Dialogues are not always between physically embodied voices, they can be between virtual or imaginary voices. Having had the experience of being questioned by others in a dialogue, children learn to appropriate that questioning voice and can question themselves when alone. Many insights occur when we are alone; after all Archimedes was alone in his bathtub when he shouted 'Eureka'! But such insights still occur in the space of dialogue between two voices. We often refer to this as 'talking to ourselves'. But actually when we question ourselves we are taking the perspective of another person so I think of this as more like talking to the Other or perhaps this is talking to 'oneself as another'.[v]

Sometimes the 'other' that people talk to when they are alone is a specific person. People often describe imagining the voice of their mother or father or a teacher questioning their ideas or actions. In the USA there are many tattoos and car stickers with the logo WWJD, meaning 'What Would Jesus Do?'. Sometimes this inner voice is not specific but is a generalized other person. To develop a really convincing argument it helps to try and imagine every possible objection from every possible kind of audience. Rather than running through all the types of audience we can think of we develop a capacity to project the perspective of the outside in general. This is the ideal of someone who does not share our prejudices and limitations but can see things clearly from all points of view. To see things through fresh eyes some use the device of 'What would a Martian think?'. That helps creativity. To see things as clearly and rationally as possible it also helps to project a wise witness position. I called this the voice of the 'infinite other' because it is a position that is always beyond us, seeing further than we can and calling us out into thinking.

Bakhtin points out that learning from dialogues is always a kind of augmentation. When we really learn from someone else we learn to see the world through a different pair of eyes. It is seldom the case that what we learn means that we have to reject our initial view and replace it completely with a new one. Dialogic learning more often means adding to our range of possible ways of seeing the world. Dialogic learning is not a journey from A to B but a journey from A to A and B.

In a similar way the dialogic theory of thinking and teaching thinking that I have developed in this book is not a rejection of Vygotskian socio-cultural theory but an augmentation of it. Every dialogue has two poles. On the one hand every dialogue is situated culturally, socially and historically. On the other hand every dialogue opens up a dialogic space which is potentially infinite. I might be talking to my son in the kitchen over breakfast at a particular place and time with all the cultural assumptions of that place and time but we can talk about distant stars and about the Big Bang at the beginning of time, we can talk about New Zealand and Alaska, about the ancient Greeks and about the cyber-civilization of the future. In fact we often do. Our situation does not limit our possibilities; being 'here and now' is precisely what enables us to be everywhere and forever.[vi]

Socio-cultural theory that claims that thinking is just a matter of using cultural tools can be in danger of a reduction of human possibilities. On the other hand socio-cultural theory is right to stress the important role of cultural tools in opening up spaces for thinking and resourcing those spaces with tools like concept words that enable thinking to take flight. Looking at the Thinking Together approach to teaching thinking we can see that ways of using language can open up possibilities for creative and critical thinking. Asking open questions is crucial for stimulating thinking and it is a culturally specific way of using words that can be taught. My point is only that what is learnt is not simply how to repeat words in the right order, what is learnt is how to use words as surfboards in the infinite space of possibilities opened up by dialogue.

Words and dialogue

If you sprinkle iron filings on a white piece of paper and then hold a magnet underneath this then the iron filings will shift and reform along the lines of force of the magnetic field. The relationship between words and the flow of meaning in dialogic space is a bit like the relationship between iron filings and the underlying magnetic field. The filings line up and 'make sense' but the sense that they make is to point us to an underlying force field that they do not contain or limit. Words only mean in the context of relationships that call us to think. This includes the central relationship we all have with the infinite other, whether we like this or not, whenever we find ourselves called forth into thinking. Just as we can see the iron filings but we cannot see the force field that motivates them so we can hear the words and even see them if they are written, but we cannot see the underlying dialogic space that motivates them and gives them meaning. Nor can we ever see the witness position or infinite other, judging between voices and seeking to understand, but this ideal, coloured in different ways in different cultural contexts, is always implicit whenever conversation turns from social chit-chat into shared enquiry.

Ground rules for using language, like asking reflective questions, are not themselves 'thinking', but they serve to open a dialogic space for thinking. Children who think creatively have not only internalized a set of words and rules but also a dialogic space and with this an infinite other, characterized by an unlimited potential for making new meaning.

How children learn to think

As I mentioned in Chapter 1, when I observed the very first Philosophy for Children lesson with a group of 5-year-olds I was struck by how much they seemed to live in their own worlds and not really listen to each other. The teacher introduced the rule of always following on from the previous speaker saying things like 'I agree with x' or 'I disagree with x' and giving reasons. Within a few sessions they were really discussing issues together.

I think that this story of how individual small perspectives become drawn into a larger dialogue provides a model of learning to think in general. When children are led to reflect on experience they are bringing moments of time together into one space where they can illuminate each other. For example, a child who understands that 5+3 is the same as 3+5 comes to this understanding only after doing both procedures and then comparing them together and seeing the similarity. By encouraging children to discuss, reflect and generally think about things we are leading them to bring isolated moments of experience together into larger dialogues.

Thinking begins with the need for children to explain themselves. However, as they explain themselves to someone else they also listen to their own voice as if in the position of another to themselves. This new other is like a witness to every dialogue. This sense of there being a witness or super-addressee leads children to question their own explanations even if the people they are actually talking to do not. I call this witness position in dialogues the infinite other because it cannot be pinned down or contained but always moves beyond any position. In dialogue with the infinite other children make sense of experience and develop their understanding even without prompting or stimulus from teachers, parents or peers. Of course this shift of thinking into a kind of virtual 'inner' dialogue does not mean that real dialogues become less important for learning. All teachers know that having to explain something clearly to someone else can help you to understand it for yourself.

The direction of the development of thinking is from fragmented and isolated moments of time, events which have no meaning or explanation for the child, towards making sense of things by bringing them into relationship. One can try to make sense of things in a narrow context or in a larger context. Bakhtin, a classical scholar, referred several times to the fact that seeing his own time from the perspective of ancient Greece helped him to make sense of what was happening around him. He outlined the ideal of Great Time as a sort of time or space in which all voices could enter into dialogue together and be understood. Teaching thinking means moving children from narrow time towards Great Time, from seeing things in a narrow context with few perspectives and few possibilities, to seeing things in a bigger context with more perspectives and more possibilities.

In Chapter 2 I talked about the shift from disputational and cumulative ways of talking towards more exploratory and dialogic ways of talking, as a shift in identity or identification. Another way of looking at this is as the development of a disposition to be dialogic. The point about calling it a shift in identity is that it seems to be identity commitments that often prevent real dialogue breaking out because people feel defensive of some image of themselves or of their group that they do not want to have exposed to questioning. The point of calling it a disposition is that it is not enough to know intellectually that you ought to question things and enter into dialogue with people and ideas, it is necessary for this to become part of who you are. To shift towards becoming more dialogic is to shift towards feeling more at home in a space of dialogue with multiple voices and no certainties.

Every area of knowledge can be taught as a dialogue

There is no point in teaching facts outside of dialogues. Every so-called 'fact' is actually an answer to a question. Teaching facts without a dialogic context that children can relate to is not teaching for understanding. But this is not a problem because every area can be taught as a dialogue. As well as the concept of 'dialogic space' as a general opening of an infinite potential for meaning, there are many smaller dialogic spaces or 'fields of dialogue' in different areas. A field of dialogue can be characterized by positions and arguments about claims. The Concept Cartoon approach to teaching science demonstrates that every scientific fact can be taught through exploring the dialogue between a range of alternatives as well as by conducting the experiments that would help us to distinguish between these alternatives.

If you put a coat on the snowman will it melt faster or slower? John says it will warm him up and melt him faster, Samira says it will block the sun's rays and so keep him cool, Holly says it will make no difference. How can we devise an experiment to find out who is right?

This approach has been developed in science but it can be applied in any area. Facts on their own do not make much sense. By teaching each area as a dialogue, indeed as a kind of dialogic space, you are also teaching children how to engage in the dialogue and how to understand for themselves. In other words by teaching every content area as a bit of dialogic space, a field of dialogue, you are also teaching children how to think and drawing them deeper into dialogue as an end in itself.

Types of thinking

So far I have talked about different aspects of good thinking but not made it very clear how creative thinking is related to critical thinking and how both are related to the idea of communication or of responsiveness within a relationship. The best answer that I have is developed from Matthew Lipman's account of thinking in the Philosophy for Children programme.[vii] Lipman wrote that good thinking always has a critical dimension and a creative dimension and also a 'caring' dimension. By caring he did not just mean empathy for other people but also engagement with areas. If you do not really care about a topic it is difficult to discuss it in depth.

I agree with Lipman that human thinking, because it is dialogic, is always creative as well as critical. It is more creative when exploring a wide range of possibilities or trying to develop a completely new design. It is more critical when the focus is on ap-plying criteria of judgement to criticize a proposal or to select between alternatives. But because it is dialogic human thought also always takes place within relationships. This means that there is always also a dimension of responsibility – meaning an obligation to respond to the needs of the other. This is what motivates reason in the first place as a need to justify, explain and generally persuade others to see things from our point of view, while respecting and seeking to understand their point of view. But beyond relationships with specific others there is a responsibility we feel in relation to cultural voices representing communities and even the future. For example, the accountable talk approach to teaching thinking stresses the need to be accountable to the norms and ideals of a community. Bakhtin describes how engaging in dialogue with a specific other also engages us in a relationship with the witness position or what he called the 'super-addressee' (I prefer the term 'infinite other' but the idea is similar). Bakhtin's super-addressee is not a real person but a kind of necessary ideal projected by dialogues. He writes that every age and culture will understand this position differently. For some it is 'God', but for others it is 'the community of science' or the 'judgement of the future'.

Real thinking draws us into relationship with someone who is always beyond us. This might sound odd but it is true to experience. In Chapter 5 I described a group of children who only managed to solve their problem when they looked at their graph from the point of view of the future addressee, the audience that they were making the graph for. Thinking is like entering into a relationship of responsibility with an unknown other. No wonder so many people find thinking a bit scary. That sense of responsibility to the other in the inner dialogues of thought often takes the form of a challenge to be truthful.

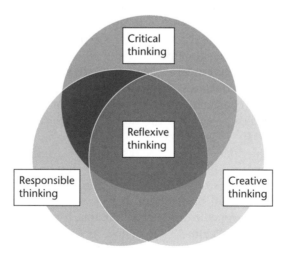

Figure 8.1 Varieties of thinking

Figure 8.1 suggests that the 'higher order thinking' described in Chapter 1 that we want to promote, has dimensions of criticality, creativity and responsibility. In each case it is possible to be critical, creative or responsible without really thinking. Computers can do rigorous deductive critical thinking without any reflection at all. There are techniques that can support creativity by generating random alternatives, which need involve no critical thinking or responsibility. And it is possible to feel responsible for something without critical or creative reflective thought.

This diagram for types of thinking mimics the chart of primary colours and I think that is entirely appropriate. There are an infinite number of different shades and varieties of colour in experience and there is an infinite variety of types of thought. In many languages colours are not easily separated from the things that possess the colour, just as in English oranges (the fruit) are orange (the colour) and turquoise (the stone) is turquoise (the colour). On the whole, after Newton's demonstration with a prism, most people accept that there is such a thing as pure light and primary colours independent of our words and our particular cultural practices. As I pointed out in the introduction the same cannot yet be said for thought. Some people still argue that it can be reduced to ways of using language and induction into cultural practices.[viii] And it is true that the kind of thinking that is valued and that we call 'good thinking' or 'higher order thinking' does vary over time and with culture. However, this does not mean that thought is not real. The evidence from successful teaching thinking programmes suggests that thought is real and can be promoted. However, this evidence points to the fact that thought cannot be a kind of computer algorithm or even a particular function of an isolated brain: from the evidence, the essence of thought appears to be reflexion or seeing as if from the point of view of another. This is something that arises within dialogic relationships and, indeed, always remains within dialogic relationships. Although language appears to be an important carrier for thought and can be used as a tool to stimulate thinking by opening spaces of reflection, the real medium of thought is intersubjectivity, or our ability to see things as if from the eyes of another. Intersubjectivity precedes and motivates language, both in evolution and in the life of a child. According to what we see in classrooms it also exceeds language, carrying children to insights and understanding beyond what they have the words to express.

Reflexive dialogical thinking is what I would call 'good thinking' or that kind of thinking that parents and educators ought to promote. It combines creativity, criticality and responsibility. It is characterized by the wisdom that comes from knowing that there is always an outside perspective that would see things differently and probably laugh at our theories, the playfulness that comes from valuing multiplicity and the enriched understanding that can come from seeing through many eyes at once.

Where is the mind?

In Chapter 1 I offered the thought experiment of a girl having her brain scanned while reading William Blake's poem 'The Tyger'. I pointed out that no amount of information on neuronal firings could tell us anything useful about her understanding of the meaning of the poem. Individual neuronal activity is obviously correlated with thought in an interesting way but it is at best a reflection of a larger flow of meaning that is more truly located in dialogues than in individual brains. To understand her response to the poem and use this to develop deeper thinking we need to be inside the dialogue with her and with Blake. Mind is not best thought of as an individual attribute or as an attribute of society. It is best thought of as an attribute of dialogues which are always both individual and social, both inside and outside, both situated and infinite, all at once.

Education as mind expansion

In the cognitive tradition mind has been compared to the software of a computer with the brain as the hardware. This is a fundamental misunderstanding. Mind is about awareness, not about rule-governed procedures like those of a computer program. We can see this in old phrases like 'minding the baby'. Awareness comes from seeing things as if through the eyes of another. We have seen in this book that it is very easy to expand mind. Simply asking 'Why?' can force children to reflect in a way that increases their awareness of what they are doing and can lead to insight and understanding. That, in its own small way, is mind expansion. All the teaching thinking programmes described in this book work by joining separate voices together into larger dialogues. This too is about mind expansion but it goes further than any physical individual. Thought, it turns out, does not exist alone in a solitary brain but is like a spark arcing out between people in relationship. Language and other, newer, communications technologies can support thinking by opening new spaces for dialogue where dialogue did not exist before, widening those spaces by bringing in new voices and deepening those spaces with supports for awareness and reflection.

Teaching for thinking and creativity expands individual children's minds to help them thrive in the more global and networked world of the future. Teaching for thinking and creativity also has a larger mission: expanding mindfulness in general to help ensure that the world of the future is a place worth thriving in.

Chapter Summary

This book gathers together some of the best practice in teaching for thinking and creativity. As well as offering summaries of research on teaching thinking and examples of good practice it develops an argument about what thinking really is. These two strands are connected. The evidence suggests that the biggest influence on the thinking of children in a classroom is the model offered by their teacher. In other words, to teach thinking effectively teachers have to think for themselves. My arguments about thinking are not meant to provide neat answers so much as to draw readers into thinking about thinking.

While this book draws on insights from philosophy and psychology its central argument is educational. In a sense every act of teaching is a kind of experiment testing out a theory of learning. Teachers and educational researchers are in a privileged position to observe how children really learn to think. The evidence from successful teaching thinking programmes does not fit very well with existing metaphors for thinking. It does not confirm the mechanism metaphor of Piaget and cognitive psychology nor does it entirely support the 'cultural tool use' metaphor behind socio-cultural theory.

Successful teaching for thinking cannot be entirely explained through references to underlying mechanisms or to cultural tool use. It is more centrally about the quality of relationships and about drawing children into dialogue.

The metaphor of thinking as dialogue and so the idea that learning to think is about being drawn into dialogue, emerges clearly from the evidence of successful primary classroom practice. Philosophy for Children and the Thinking Together approach teach thinking by drawing children into dialogue supporting this with structured teaching of 'ground rules' and types of language use. Anna Craft's account of teaching for creativity is about supporting children's 'What if' questioning to open up spaces of possibility. Guy Claxton's approach to Building Learning Power structures environments and activities to promote essential dialogic dispositions like responsiveness, reflection and resilience.

In this book I have tried to explore what taking a dialogic perspective means for education. Dialogic is more than just the description of actual dialogues. Dialogues lead to the opening of dialogic space: a space of multiplicity, uncertainty and potentiality. This dialogic space is paradoxical because it is the idea of an inclusive boundary. One way to understand this is to think about the way in which, for each participant in a dialogue, the voice of the other is an outside perspective that includes them within it. An utterance in a dialogue already presupposes an orientation towards the response of the other person. The boundary between selves is not therefore a demarcation line, or an external link between self and other, but an inclusive 'space' of dialogue within which self and other mutually construct, de-construct and re-construct each other. The dialogic principle is a principle of non-identity or of outside-inness and inside-outness. Although the dialogue metaphor comes from actual dialogues between people the dialogic principle applies to thinking more generally.

Thinking dialogues are not only limited to dialogues with other children and with teachers and parents but they can also occur with more abstract kinds of partner. Every dialogue generates a witness position from which we can question and reflect back on what we are saying. However, our own reflective dialogue with this witness position also generates its own witness position and so on in a way that cannot be contained. There is therefore a kind of infinite potential for new questioning and for new ways of seeing implicit in every dialogue. Most dialogues occur with a finite other in a finite context for a fixed purpose, but they all nonetheless have an infinite potential for creative reflection. It is the job of the teacher to activate some of that potential. Teaching thinking therefore involves drawing children more into relationship with the infinite other who is already implicit in dialogue. It is about opening children up to the call of thinking.

Teaching for thinking and creativity can be quite simply understood as teaching for dialogue as an end in itself. The less we identify with fixed images and the more we identify with dialogue the more creative we are and the more we are really thinking.

My discussion of learning to think has been supported by insights from philosophy such as Heidegger's account of thinking as a response to a call and Merleau-Ponty's notion of the 'inside out: outside in' chiasm at the heart of consciousness. I have also incorporated insights from psychology such as Vygotsky's account of learning to think as internalizing dialogues and Csíkszentmihályi's notion of 'flow'. However, the dialogic theory of how to teach for thinking that I develop here remains a distinctly educational theory grounded on the reality of classroom practice. It is derived from understanding which educational activities really work and then trying to figure out, through experiment and reflection, why exactly it is that they work. As an educational theory, in turn, this dialogic theory has implications for practice. **One implication is that teaching for understanding requires a dialogic approach. All more specific areas of knowledge should therefore be taught not as facts but as fields of dialogue**. This can be done in every area, in science, history, maths, RE etc., through actively engaging children in asking the questions and developing the arguments that created the field of knowledge in the first place and that can help the children recreate for themselves. Suggestions of how to do this are given in the book as well as references to further resources. Another implication is that effective teaching for thinking and learning tends towards engaging children in dialogues that take them beyond the classroom walls. Dialogic education works to expand the mind by bringing previously isolated moments of experience into relationship. **This process of mind expansion does not stop with the individual or with the classroom but requires that education becomes a driver towards more global dialogue and more global awareness**. In my view it is to support this need to draw children into global dialogues that ICT most comes into its own as an indispensable tool to support teaching thinking.

Finally, in trying to persuade you of my argument I notice that I have slipped into an authoritative tone at times, as if I had found out all the answers. However, the dialogic theory of education that I put forward in this book is meant to be a truly *dialogic* theory. This means that it is intended only as a provisional contribution to an ongoing dialogue. I enjoyed exploring the difficult questions of thinking, creativity and dialogic that I raised in this book, but I do not claim to have fully understood them or to have given more than a partial and temporary answer to them. My hope is that this book will stimulate you to think with me and to think beyond me. After all, **the evidence is clear that to be an effective teacher of thinking it is not at all necessary to have a correct theory; it is much more important to enjoy thinking and to communicate that joy to others**.

Glossary

Chiasm: this is the idea from philosopher Merleau-Ponty, that there are two sides to every perception and every thought. In thinking, he claims, there is always an inside looking out and an outside looking in. We can see from one side or from the other but we can never see from both sides at once. That is why we can never grasp the whole truth.

Consciousness: seeing as if through the eyes of another. Just to see things and get a neurological reaction does not imply consciousness. In becoming conscious we learn to see things as if we were another person to ourselves and so we are able to describe what we see and question it, and think it could be different from what it is.

Creative thinking: all thinking has an element of creativity but specifically creative thinking is that kind of thinking that comes up with surprising new ideas.

Creativity: the skill of coming up with a good new idea when you need one.

Creativity 1: making new associations in an almost random way because there is something, anything at all, that is similar between the associated things so that the one thing calls the other thing to mind. In classroom activities creativity 1 is found in the 'brainstorming' or 'thought shower' stage of a class discussion.

Creativity 2: fashioning a socially valued product. This product could be a thing, like a sculpture, or an idea. In classroom activities creativity 2 is associated with the phase after brainstorming when useful ideas are selected and developed to provide the best possible answer to a question.

Critical thinking: all thinking has an element of criticality but specifically critical thinking focuses on judgement in order to select the good ideas from the bad ones.

Dialogic: the principle of holding different voices or perspectives together in creative tension. Dialogic is a contrasting term to monologic: monologic assumes that there is just one voice, perspective or truth but for dialogic there is always more than one voice, perspective or truth.

Dialogic space: when two or more voices are held together in the tension of a dialogue this opens up a space of possible responses. In dialogic space children and teachers can co-construct new ideas together or stimulate each other to provoke creative and unexpected responses.

Dialogic talk: engaged, responsive, creative, open-ended shared enquiry. Talk together can be more or less dialogic. The more dialogic it is, the more it is characterized by active listening and the creative emergence of new ideas.

Dialogue: this is often used to refer to any conversation but Bakhtin makes a useful distinction between dialogue and conversation, defining dialogue as a shared enquiry in which each answer produces a further question in a chain of questions and answers.

Difference: there are two kinds of difference; ordinary difference and constitutive difference. Ordinary difference is the difference between two fixed identities, like the difference between a red cup and a blue cup. Constitutive difference is where the difference between two identities helps to define the identities of the two things from within. So, for example, the difference between me and you in a dialogue is at least partly constitutive, because I can't have a 'me' without a 'you' and you also can't have a 'you' without a 'me' so it is the difference between us that helps to define us.

Exploratory Talk: characterized by Neil Mercer as thinking together where the 'reasoning is visible in the talk'. Research has shown such talk to be very valuable but also that it is related to the nature of tasks. In some creative tasks, where there are many possible solutions, the most effective kind of talk does not display explicit reasoning. This is why we need the broader category of dialogic talk.

Flow: the experience of engagement in creative work where the identification is on both sides at once so that the work feels pulled as much as it feels pushed. Flow is the product of chiasmic relationships with people and with domains of culture.

Identity: any bit of reality or experience that we can put a boundary around and refer to as a thing.

Infinite other: in this book I develop Bakhtin's idea of the super-addressee into the idea of the 'infinite other'. When we are alone and not actually talking to someone else but we are thinking this implies that we take on the position of an 'other' person to ourselves. That 'other' could be a very specific image of someone, like my dad, or it could be the more open idea of trying to see things as if from the outside, perhaps even taking a 'Martian's eye view' of things. The infinite other is infinite only in the sense of not being limited or bounded or pindownable.

Knowledge age skills: the skills, habits and dispositions that people will need to thrive when the global economy is dominated by the production, distribution and consumption of knowledge rather than of material goods. These skills combine more traditional 'thinking skills' such as creativity and problem solving with skills such as cross-cultural understanding and the effective use of new media to communicate and to collaborate.

Mind: consciousness. To mind something is to be aware of it. To remind someone of something helps them to remember it. To remember something is to bring it back into the dialogue. It is as if a member of the meeting has wandered away and needs to be recalled so that they can add their voice. Expanding the mind is bringing previously separate voices or fragments of experience into dialogue with one another.

Reason: critical thought. Because of its origins in the Greek word 'ratio' the word reason refers more to measurement and to judgement than to creativity and so is a synonym for critical thought.

Responsibility: being called to respond to the needs of the other in the context of a relationship.

Socio-cultural: this term has at least two meanings, one broad and one quite narrow. The broad meaning simply refers to the fact that all thinking is situated in a historical, cultural and social context. A dialogic perspective on thinking accepts this but argues that dialogues open up a space of possibilities from which people can question, challenge and sometimes transform their contexts. To put this another way: while it is true that dialogues are situated within cultures it is also true that how we interpret any culture is from within dialogues.

The narrower meaning of the term socio-cultural is the tradition from Vygotsky claiming that thinking is always mediated by cultural tools such as language. Sometimes this can provide useful insights but, from a dialogic perspective, it is ultimately reductionist. From a dialogic perspective thinking is rooted in intersubjectivity rather than in language use. Thinking is first about seeing things from the other's point of view and only second about using words or signs. It is this intersubjectivity, when applied to dialogue with the infinite other, that enables thought to transcend specific cultural contexts.

Super-addressee: Bakhtin claimed that in any dialogue, as well as the actual person or people you are talking to, the addressee or addressees, there is also an imaginary third party or 'witness'. He referred to this third party as the 'super-addressee'. The super-addressee is the ideal of the sort of person who can understand what you are trying to say even when no one else can.

Thinking: dialogue. This could be dialogue with real other people talking together in a room, dialogue with imaginary other people or dialogue with the infinite other.

Notes

Chapter 1 Is it really possible to teach 'thinking'?

i. G. Claxton (2008) *What is the Point of School?* London: Oneworld Publications.
ii. One example of a critic of teaching thinking is J. McPeck (1981) *Critical Thinking and Education*. New York: St. Martin's Press. Many philosophers of education agree with McPeck. See, for example, S. Johnson and P. Gardner (1999) Some Achilles heels of thinking skills: A response to Higgins and Baumfield. *Journal of Philosophy of Education*, 33(3), 435–449.
iii. See D. N. Perkins and G. Salomon (1989) Are cognitive skills context bound? *Educational Researcher*, 18(1), 16–25.
iv. R. J. Sternberg (1990) *Metaphors of Mind: Conceptions of the nature of intelligence*. New York: Cambridge University Press, p 13.
v. S. J. Blakemore and U. Frith (2005) *The Learning Brain: Lessons for education*. Oxford: Blackwell.
vi. A. Smith (1998) *Accelerated Learning: Brain-based methods for accelerating motivation and achievement*. London: Network Educational Press.
vii. M. Velmans (2000) *Understanding Consciousness*. London: Routledge.
viii. A. Edwards (2005) Let's get beyond community and practice: The many meanings of learning by participating. *The Curriculum Journal*, 16(1), 49–65.
ix. N. Mercer and K. Littleton (2007) *Dialogue and the Development of Children's Thinking: A sociocultural approach*. London: Routledge. See also R. Wegerif, N. Mercer and L. Dawes (1999) From social interaction to individual reasoning: An empirical investigation of a possible sociocultural model of cognitive development. *Learning and Instruction*, 9(5), 493–516.
x. M. Heidegger (1978) *Basic Writings*. London: Routledge, p 390.
xi. L. Resnick (1987) *Education and Learning to Think*. Washington, DC: National Academy Press.
xii. R. Wegerif (2003) *Thinking Skills, Technology and Learning: A review of the literature*. Bristol: NESTA FutureLab. http://www.nestafuturelab.org
xiii. P. Adey and M. Shayer (1994) *Really Raising Standards*. London: Routledge.
xiv. P. Adey (ed.) (2008) *Let's Think Handbook: Cognitive Acceleration in the Primary School*. London: nferNelson.
xv. R. Wegerif, J. Perez Linares, S. Rojas Drummond, N. Mercer and M. Velez (2005) Thinking Together in the UK and Mexico: Transfer of an educational innovation. *Journal of Classroom Interaction*, 40(1), 40–47.

xvi. R. Wegerif and N. Mercer (2000) Language for thinking. In H. Cowie, D. Aalsvoort, and N. Mercer (eds) *New Perspectives in Collaborative Learning*. Oxford: Elsevier.

xvii. K. Topping and S. Trickey (2007) Collaborative Philosophical Enquiry for School Children: Cognitive Effects at 10–12 Years. *British Journal of Educational Psychology*, 77(2), 271–288.

xviii. R. Alexander (ed.) (2009) *Children, their World, their Education: Final report and recommendations of the Cambridge Review*. London: Routledge, p 306.

xix. M. Sendak (1963) *Where the Wild Things Are*. Harmondsworth: Puffin Books (now a movie).

xx. *Philosophy For Children*, Level 1 Manual available from SAPERE http://www.sapere.org.uk

Chapter 2   What is Dialogic Education?

i. R. Alexander (ed.) (2009) *Children, their World, their Education: Final report and recommendations of the Cambridge Review*. London: Routledge, p 306.

ii. Much of this work appears in R. Wegerif and P. Scrimshaw (eds) (1998) *Computers and Talk in the Primary Classroom*. Clevedon, UK: Multilingual Matters.

iii. Lyn Dawes, Neil Mercer and myself.

iv. Three months was long enough for them to forget the original question and we used control groups doing the same tests three months apart to show that the improvement we saw was not simply a product of maturation.

v. Previously published in R. Wegerif and L. Dawes (2004) *Thinking and Learning with ICT: Raising achievement in primary classrooms*. London: Routledge.

vi. This is a parallel problem to Raven's B12 prepared for publication with the permission of Dr John Raven who holds the copyright for Raven's Reasoning Tests.

vii. The full transcript of one group of 9-year-old children (whom we called Tara, Perry and Keira) working on a version of the problem shown in Figure 2.1, in a pre-test and again in a post-test, is published in Wegerif and Dawes (2004), pp 37–39.

viii. R. Alexander (2000) *Culture and Pedagogy*. Oxford: Blackwell.
Another source for the term dialogic in UK education whom I should mention was Gordon Wells whose 1986 book showing the importance of drawing children into rich conversations, *The Meaning Makers*, was very influential. He later articulated this in terms of 'dialogic' in his 1999 book *Dialogic Inquiry: Towards a socio-cultural practice and theory of education*.

ix. See http://www.robinalexander.org.uk/dialogicteaching.htm

x. See L. Dawes (2008) *The Essential Speaking and Listening: Talk for learning at Key Stage 2*. London: Routledge. Also R. J. Alexander (2006) *Education as Dialogue: Moral and pedagogical choices for a runaway world*. Cambridge: Dialogos, 37–43.

xi. R. Wegerif, J. Perez Linares, S. Rojas Drummond, N. Mercer and M. Velez (2005) Thinking Together in the UK and Mexico: Transfer of an educational innovation. *Journal of Classroom Interaction*, 40(1), 40–47.

xii. K. Topping and S. Trickey (2007) Collaborative Philosophical Enquiry for School Children: Cognitive Effects at 10–12 Years. *British Journal of Educational Psychology*, 77(2), 271–288.

xiii. M. Bakhtin (1986) *Speech Genres and Other Late Essays*. Austin: University of Texas Press, p 161.

xiv. G. Leibniz (1973) *Leibniz: Philosophical Writings* (G. Parkinson (ed.), trans. M. Morris and G. Parkinson). London: Dent and Sons, p 206.

xv. M. Bakhtin (1981) *The Dialogic Imagination*. Austin: University of Texas Press, p 343.

xvi. J. Rose (2009) *Independent Review of the Primary Curriculum: Final report* available on http://www.dcsf.gov.uk/primarycurriculumreview/ and R. Alexander (ed.) (2009) *Children, their World, their Education: Final report and recommendations of the Cambridge Review*. London: Routledge.

xvii. See S. Pinker (1998) *How the Mind Works*. Harmondsworth: Penguin, for an excellent summary of this approach to understanding the mind.

xviii. R. P. Hobson (2002) *The Cradle of Thought: Exploring the origins of thinking*. London: Macmillan.

xix. L. E. Crandell and R. P. Hobson (1999) Individual Differences in Young Children's IQ: A social-developmental perspective. *Journal of Child Psychology and Psychiatry*, 40, 455–464.

xx. M. Tomasello, M. Carpenter, J. Call, T. Behne and H. Moll (2005) Understanding and Sharing Intentions: The origins of cultural cognition. *Behavior and Brain Science*, 28(5), 675–691.

xxi. Ibid.

xxii. This should be seen as developing socio-cultural theory further from within rather than as a rejection of it. Vygotsky and neo-Vygotskians tend to focus on sign-tools and how children internalize these sign-tools. The small additional step I am taking is to focus on the 'dialogic space' that is required first if signs are to have any meaning. Learning to think involves internalizing this 'dialogic space' as well as the sign-tools.

xxiii. A good review of the evidence is provided in M. Tomasello et al., op. cit.

xxiv. This has not always been the case. Introspection was an important method in the early days of psychology with Wilhelm Wundt and William James.

xxv. M. Heidegger (1978) *Basic Writings*. London: Routledge, p 369.

xxvi. Ibid., p 391.

xxvii. S. Hand (2009) *Emmanuel Levinas*. London: Routledge.

xxviii. See http://thinkingtogether.educ.cam.ac.uk/ and L. Dawes, N. Mercer and R. Wegerif (2000) *Thinking Together: A programme of activities for developing speaking, listening and thinking skills for children aged 8–11*. Birmingham: Imaginative Minds Ltd.

xxix. This crucial point is the fruit of experience but it is also confirmed by rigorous quantitative research showing that the main influence on the way in which children talk together in any classroom is the way in which their teachers talk with them: N. M. Webb, K. M. Nemer and M. Ing (2006) Small-group reflections: Parallels between teacher discourse and student behavior in peer-directed groups. *Journal of the Learning Sciences*, 15(1), 63–119.

xxx. R. Wegerif and L. Dawes (2004), op. cit.

xxxi. L. Dawes (2008), op. cit.

xxxii. S. Wolfe (2006) Teaching and learning through dialogue in primary classrooms in England. Unpublished PhD thesis, University of Cambridge, pp 258–259. See also her paper in *Beyond Current Horizons*: http://www.beyondcurrenthorizons.org.uk

Chapter 3 Creative talk

i. B. S. Bloom (ed.) (1956) *Taxonomy of Educational Objectives: The classification of educational goals: Handbook I, Cognitive Domain.* New York; Toronto: Longmans, Green.

ii. L. Anderson and D. Krathwohl (2001) *A taxonomy for learning, teaching, and assessing.* New York: Longman.

iii. NACCCE (1999) *All our Futures: Creativity, culture and education: National Advisory Committee on Creative and Cultural Education.* London: DfEE and DCMS, p 29.

iv. It might be thought that this distinction is the same as the distinction made between capital 'C' creativity and small 'c' creativity by Csíkszentmihályi and other writers on creativity including Anna Craft, but actually it is different as I am proposing a temporal and logical relationship between creativity 1 and creativity 2: creativity 2 depends upon and fashions creativity 1. Creativity with a small 'c' versus creativity with a capital 'C' is different as the distinction is about social recognition. Creativity with a small 'c' is reserved for the kind of creativity displayed by everyday activities like cooking or flower arranging whereas Creativity with a big 'C' is reserved for creativity that has social and historical recognition as truly original and so taking a field of human endeavour further forward.

I do not find the distinction between big 'C' and little 'c' creativity very useful for the average classroom whereas the distinction between creativity 1 and creativity 2 is essential as it is the difference between a 'thought shower' phase where all ideas are valued, however wacky, (creativity 1) and a phase of selection of the best ideas and their development into something presentable like a poster or website (creativity 2).

v. N. Mercer (1995) *The Guided Construction of Knowledge: Talk amongst teachers and learners.* Clevedon: Multilingual Matters.

vi. R. Carter (1999) Common language: Corpus, creativity and cognition. *Language and Literature*, 8(3), 195–216; R. Carter (2002) *Language and Creativity.* London: Routledge.

vii. N. Mercer ibid., p 101.

viii. M. Sendak (1963) *Where the Wild Things Are.* Harmondsworth: Puffin Books (now a movie).

ix. T. Kuhn (1962) *The Structure of Scientific Revolutions*. Chicago: University of Chicago Press.

x. A similar word, 'fantabulosa', is found in dictionaries of 'polari', British gay slang from the 1960s, but I am convinced that it was a new word to these girls.

xi. K. Dunbar (1997) How scientists think: On-line creativity and conceptual change in science. In T. B. Ward, S. M. Smith and J. Vaid (eds) *Creative Thought: An investigation of conceptual structures and processes*. Washington, DC: American Psychological Association, p 13. I am influenced here by K. Sawyer (2006) *Explaining Creativity: The science of human innovation*. New York: Oxford University Press, and K. Sawyer (2007) *Group Genius: The creative power of collaboration*. New York: Basic Books.

xii. W. Gordon (1961) *Synectics*. New York: Harper and Row.

xiii. A. Craft (2005) *Creativity in Schools: Tensions and dilemmas*. London: Routledge.

xiv. G. Claxton, L. Edwards and V. Scale-Constantinou (2006) Cultivating creative mentalities: A framework for education. *Thinking Skills and Creativity*, 1(1), 57–61.

xv. P. Burnard, T. Grainger and A. Craft (2006) Documenting possibility thinking: A journey of collaborative enquiry. *International Journal of Early Years Education*, Special Issue on *Creativity and Cultural Innovation in Early Childhood Education*, 14(3), 243–262.

xvi. T. Grainger, P. Burnard and A. Craft (2006) Pedagogy and possibility thinking in the Early Years. *Thinking Skills and Creativity*, 1(2), 26–38.

xvii. R. Ritchhart and D. Perkins (2005) Learning to think: The challenges of teaching thinking. In K. Holyoak and R. G. Morrison (eds) *Cambridge Handbook of Thinking and Reasoning*. Cambridge: Cambridge University Press.

xviii. See M. De Boo (1999) *Using Science to Develop Thinking Skills at Key Stage 1*. London: National Association for Able Children in Education/David Fulton.

xix. See A. Peat (2001) Creative Teaching. *Teaching Thinking*, Issue 5 (Autumn), 50–51.

xx. Adapted from R. Fisher's site: http://www.teachingthinking.net/

xxi. D. Faulkner, M. Joubert and S. Kynan (2006) *Project EXCITE!: Excellence, creativity and innovation in teaching and education Phase II: A longitudinal study of excellence, creativity and innovation in teaching and learning in primary education*. http://www.excite-education.org/

Chapter 4   Creative understanding

i. M. Chi (1997) Creativity: Shifting across ontological categories flexibly. In T. B. Ward, S. M. Smith and J. Vaid (eds) *Creative Thought: An investigation of conceptual structures and processes* (p. 209–234). Washington, DC: American Psychological Association.

  See also the more recent statement of the same theory of conceptual change in M. Chi and S. Brem (2009) Contrasting Ohlsson's Resubsumption Theory With Chi's Categorical Shift Theory. *Educational Psychologist*, 44(1), 58–63.

ii. M. Gladwell (2008) *Outliers: The story of success*. New York: Little, Brown and Company.

iii. J. Wertsch and S. Kazak (2010) Saying more than you know in instructional setting. In T. Koschmann (ed.) *Theorizing Practice: Theories of learning and research into instructional practice*. New York: Springer.

iv. M. Merleau-Ponty (1964) *Signs* (trans. Richard McCleary). Evanston, IL: Northwestern University Press, p 46.

v. J. Geirland (1996) Go With The Flow. *Wired Magazine*, September, Issue 4.09.

vi. M. Csíkszentmihályi (1996) *Creativity: Flow and the psychology of discovery and invention*. New York: HarperCollins.

vii. Ibid.

viii. K. Sawyer (2007) *Group Genius: The creative power of collaboration*. New York: Basic Books, p 42.

ix. This is an example of the 'epistemic fallacy' reducing how we come to know something to an explanation of the thing itself. This anti-realist reasoning fallacy has been popular ever since Wittgenstein's claim that the meaning of a word is often simply how we use that word. But Wittgenstein was a real thinker, not an authority to be followed. The reduction of meaning to cultural practices is usually highly misleading and is incompatible with the findings of physical science which uncovers the hidden underlying structures of reality.

x. M. Csíkszentmihályi (1996) *Creativity: Flow and the psychology of discovery and invention*. New York: HarperCollins, p 119.

xi. Ibid., p 103.

xii. M. Heidegger (1969) *Identity and Difference* (bilingual edn, trans. J. Stambaugh). New York: Harper and Row.

xiii. M. Merleau-Ponty (1964) *Le Visible et L' Invisible*. Paris: Gallimard.

xiv. J. Derrida (1968) La Différance in: *Théorie d'ensemble*. Paris Éditions de Seuil.

xv. G. Leibniz (1973) *Leibniz: Philosophical Writings* (G. Parkinson (ed.), trans. M. Morris and G. Parkinson). London: Dent and Sons, p 206.

xvi. M. Merleau-Ponty (1964) *Le Visible et L'Invisible*. Paris: Gallimard. Also M. Merleau-Ponty (1968) *The Visible and the Invisible* (Claude Lefort (ed.), trans. Alphonso Lingis). Evanston, IL: Northwestern University Press.

xvii. I tend to take the 'transcendental realist' view that there is a real world out there but that this should not be confused with the world that we experience which is a constructed world or the world 'for us'. In this argument I am talking about the constructed world and not about the whole of reality. More on this view can be found in M. Archer, R. Bhaskar, A. Collier, A. Lawson and A. Norrie (eds) (1998) *Critical Realism: Essential readings*. London: Routledge.

xviii. T. S. Eliot (1936) 'Burnt Norton'. http://www.tristan.icom43.net/quartets/norton.html

xix. D. Wyse and P. Dowson (2009) *The Really Useful Creativity Book*. London: Routledge.

xx. See http://www.mantleoftheexpert.com/ and G. Bolton and D. Heathcote (1995) *Drama for Learning: Dorothy Heathcote's Mantle of the Expert Approach to Education* (Dimensions of Drama). London: Heinemann.

xxi. G. Claxton (2006) Thinking at the edge: Developing soft creativity. *Cambridge Journal of Education*, 36(3), 351–362.

xxii. A. Craft (2000) *Creativity across the Primary Curriculum: Framing and Developing Practice*. London: RoutledgeFalmer.

Chapter 5   Reason

i. P. Carpenter, M. Just and P. Shell (1990) What one intelligence test measures: A theoretical account of the processing of the Raven Progressive Matrices test. *Psychological Review*, 9(7), 404–431.

ii. R. Wegerif and N. Mercer (1997) Using computer-based text analysis to integrate quantitative and qualitative methods in the investigation of collaborative learning. *Language and Education*, 11(3), 27–35.

iii. The data was from the work of Richard Lehrer and Leona Schauble and this account will appear in Tim Koschmann (ed.) (in press) *Theorizing Practice*. New York: Springer, along with other interpretations of their data from a range of educational researchers and theorists.

iv. Ibid.

v. My account is probably inspired by that of George Herbert Mead but where Mead talks about the importance of entering into a relationship with the 'generalised other' which he associated with a concrete community, I argue that to really reason we need a relationship beyond any given community with the infinite other. See G. H. Mead (1934) *Mind, Self, and Society: From the Perspective of a Social Behaviorist* (edited, with an Introduction, by Charles W. Morris). Chicago: University of Chicago Press.

vi. M. Bakhtin (1986) *Speech Genres and Other Late Essays*. Austin: University of Texas, p 125.

vii. L. Vygotsky (1986) *Thought and Language* (trans. A. Kozulin). Cambridge, MA: MIT Press, p 199 and throughout.

viii. M. Bakhtin (1986) op. cit., p 126.

ix. L. Resnick, S. Michaels and C. O'Connor (in press) How (well structured) talk builds the mind. In R. Sternberg and D. Preiss (eds) *Innovations in Educational Psychology: Perspectives on learning, teaching and human development*. New York: Springer.

x. See S. Erduran, J. Osborne and S. Simon (2004) Enhancing the Quality of Argument in School Science. *Journal of Research in Science Teaching*, 41(10), 994–1020; and N. Mercer, L. Dawes, R. Wegerif and C. Sams (2004) Reasoning as a scientist: Ways of helping children to use language to learn science. *British Educational Research Journal*, 30(3), 367–385.

xi. R. Wegerif and L. Dawes (2004) *Thinking and Learning with ICT: Raising achievement in primary classrooms*. London: Routledge Falmer, p 81.

xii. N. Mercer, L. Dawes, R. Wegerif and C. Sams (2004), op. cit.

xiii. Brenda and Stuart Naylor (2000) *The Snowman's Coat and other Science Questions*. London: Hodder Children's Books.

xiv. Further information is on http://www.teachingexpertise.com/about-teaching-expertise and also http://www.puppetsproject.com/research.php; http://www.puppetsproject.com/resources.php

xv. S. Toulmin (1958) *The Uses of Argument*. Cambridge, UK: Cambridge University Press.

xvi. I ran out of space for practical ideas in this chapter. I had also wanted to return again to illustrate the work of CASE (Cognitive Acceleration in Science Education) which I had mentioned in Chapter 1 (more details can be found at http://www.edu.dudley.gov.uk/science/CASE.html) and the excellent work of Deanna Kuhn who has resources on her website at http://www.educationforthinking.org/.

Chapter 6   Thinking through the curriculum

i. D. Leat and S. Higgins (2002) The role of powerful pedagogical strategies in curriculum development. *The Curriculum Journal*, 13(1), 71–85.

ii. For further details of the application of this strategy in primary mathematics and science see S. Higgins (2001) *Thinking Through Primary Teaching*. Cambridge: Chris Kington Publishing.

iii. See S. Williams and R. Wegerif (2006) *Radical encouragement: Changing cultures of learning*. Birmingham: Imaginative Minds.

iv. D. Leat and S. Higgins, op. cit.

v. http://curriculum.qcda.gov.uk/new-primary-curriculum/essentials-for-learning-and-life/learning-and-thinking-skills/index.aspx

Chapter 7   Thinking and creativity with ICT

i. Accessed 22 December 2009 from http://www.dailymail.co.uk/femail/article-1215048/Meet-Tavi-Gevinson-13-tiny-blogger-fashion-industry-feet.html

ii. All accessible on http://www.statistics.gov.uk/

iii. This idea was also expressed by P. Levy (1999) *Collective Intelligence: Mankind's emerging world in cyberspace*. New York: Perseus.

iv. B. Trilling and P. Hood (2001) Learning, Technology and Education Reform in the Knowledge Age, or 'We're Wired, Webbed and Windowed, Now What?'. In C. Paechter, R. Edwards, R. Harrison and P. Twining (eds) *Learning, Space and Identity*. London: Paul Chapman Publishing and The Open University. Also at http://www.wested.org/cs/we/view/rs/654

v. For example, A. Bruns (2008) *Blogs, Wikipedia, Second Life, and Beyond: From production to produsage*. New York: Peter Lang.

vi. Independent ICT in School Commission (1997) *Stevenson Report*. http://rubble.heppell.net/stevenson/

vii. Scholastic, *I'm Ready for Kindergarten: Huggley's Sleepover*. http://www.tangled-web.com/scholastic/hug.htm

viii. A. Loveless (2000) Creativity, visual literacy and information and communications technology. In D. M. Watson and T. Downes (eds) *Communications and Networking in Education: Learning in a networked society*. Norwell, MA: Kluwer Academic.

ix. A. Loveless, J. Burton and K. Turvey (2006) Developing conceptual frameworks for creativity, ICT and teacher education. *Thinking Skills and Creativity*, 1(1), 1–11.

x. S. Papert (1981) *Mindstorms*. Brighton: Harvester.

xi. D. Jonassen, C. Carr and H. Yueh (1998) Computers as Mindtools for Engaging Learners in Critical Thinking. *TechTrends*, 43, 24–32.

xii. Adapted from D. Perkins and G. Salomon (1989) Are cognitive skills context bound? *Educational Researcher*, 18(1), 16–25.

xiii. M. Hughes (1990) Children's computation. In R. Grieve and M. Hughes (eds) *Understanding Children*. Oxford: Blackwell, p 133.

xiv. *Lines*, a programme by SMILE Mathematics which unfortunately stopped trading shortly after collaborating with me.

xv. Here I was working with Clare Sams, a teacher-researcher, and Jenny Housaert, a mathematics educator now at the Institute of Education in London.

xvi. R. Wegerif (1996) Using computers to help coach exploratory talk across the curriculum. *Computers and Education*, 26(1–3), 51–60.

xvii. R. Wegerif and L. Dawes (2004) *Thinking and Learning with ICT: Raising achievement in primary classrooms*. London: Routledge.

xviii. M. De Laat (2006) *Networked Learning*. Amsterdam: Politie Academy.

xix. This work is in progress but one relevant publication is R. Deaney, A. Chapman and S. Hennessy (2009) A case-study of one teacher's use of an interactive whiteboard system to support knowledge co-construction in the history classroom. *Curriculum Journal*, 20(4), 365–387.

xx. N. Mercer, R. Kershner, P. Warwick and J. Kleine Staarman (2010) Can the Interactive Whiteboard help provide 'dialogic space' for children's collaborative activity? *Language and Education*, 55(1), 350–362.

xxi. J. Ipgrave (2003) Building E-Bridges. Inter-Faith Dialogue by E-mail. *Teaching Thinking*, Summer, Issue 11.

xxii. J. Goody (1977) *The Domestication of the Savage Mind*. Cambridge, UK: Cambridge University Press.

xxiii. This is currently free to download from www.dialogbox.org.uk.

xxiv. Figure 7.3: edited still from 'Light Shifts' a multimodal PowerPoint presentation (see L. Cunliffe (2008) A Case Study: How Interdisciplinary Teaching Using Information and Communication Technology and Supported by a Creative Partner Impacted on Creativity in an Extra-Curricular School Activity. *International Journal of Education through Art*, 4(1), 91–104).

xxv. R. Wegerif, B. McLaren, M. Chamrada, O. Scheuer, N. Mansour, J. Mikšátko and M. Williams (2010) Exploring creative thinking in graphically mediated synchronous dialogues. *Computers and Education*, 54(3), 613–621. Also R. Wegerif (2007) *Dialogic, Education and Technology: Expanding the space of learning*. CSCL Series. New Jersey: Springer.

xxvi. This brief review is based on a much more extensive review published by NESTA FutureLab. R. Wegerif (2003) *Thinking Skills, Technology and Learning: A review of the literature for NESTA FutureLab*. Available at http://www.nestafuturelab.org/ papers (accessed 25 July 2009).

Chapter 8 Mind expanding

i. G. Claxton (2002) *Building Learning Power*. Bristol: TLO.
ii. Op. cit. and http://www.sofweb.vic.edu.au/edulibrary/public/teachlearn/ innovation/
iii. The National Centre for Excellence in the Teaching of Mathematics (NCETM). http://www.ncetm.org.uk/enquiry/10710
iv. S. Williams and R. Wegerif (2006) *Radical Encouragement: Changing cultures of learning*. Birmingham: Imaginative Minds, p 82.
v. P. Ricoeur (1995) *Oneself as Another*. Chicago: University of Chicago Press.
vi. This is a near quotation from M. Merleau-Ponty (1962) *The Phenomenology of Perception* (trans. Colin Smith). London: Routledge.
vii. M. Lipman (2003) *Thinking in Education* (2nd edn). Cambridge: Cambridge University Press.
viii. People often quote Wittgenstein as an authority for the view that thought is no more than the way that we choose to talk about it or the cultural practices within which we use the term. Thinking about how exactly the same arguments could be made for a term like light, or colour terms like orange, should make those who engage in this kind of naive socio-cultural reductionism pause and reflect. Just because we have a term for something, and rules for using that word, does not mean that the thing in question does not have an independent reality beyond our language and our culture.

Resources

Here are just a few links for teachers and parents who want to follow up some of the practical approaches to teaching for thinking and creativity mentioned in this book. Other links and texts are mentioned in the notes.

Philosophy for Children

Matthew Lipman founded this approach. His centre, The Institute for the Advancement of Philosophy with Children, at Montclair State University has many useful references and links: http://cehs.montclair.edu/academic/iapc/

The UK Society for Philosophy for Children, SAPERE, can provide training and resources: http://www.sapere.org.uk/

Further resources and training are available from http://www.p4c.com/ and http://www.dialogueworks.co.uk/

Thinking Together

The website http://thinkingtogether.educ.cam.ac.uk/ lists key books and has downloadable resources.

A good introduction to practice in the primary classroom is: L. Dawes, N. Mercer and R. Wegerif (2000) *Thinking Together: A programme of activities for developing speaking, listening and thinking skills for children aged 8–11*. Birmingham: Imaginative Minds Ltd.

Related materials for promoting speaking and listening for learning and thinking can be found at Debbie Myhill's 'It's Good to Talk' project page: http://education.exeter.ac.uk/itsgoodtotalk. The materials on this site introduce teachers to the key research issues on Talk for Learning and offer practical classroom strategies for teaching thinking which are founded upon the research principles. A key text for this site is: D. Myhill, S. Jones and R. Hopper (2006) *Talking, Listening, Learning: Effective talk in the primary classroom*. Open University Press.

Dialogic Teaching

Further information, reports and references can be found on http://www.robinalexander.org.uk/dialogicteaching.htm

Mantle of the Expert

Training information, research reports and ideas for teaching are available on http://www.mantleoftheexpert.com/

Concept Cartoons and Puppets

Brenda Keogh and Stuart Naylor are behind both the Concept Cartoons and the Puppets. Resources for science, maths and English can be found on: http://www.conceptcartoons.com/index_flash.html and http://www.puppetsproject.com/

Building Learning Power

The key book here is: Guy Claxton (2002) *Building Learning Power: Helping young people become better learners*. Bristol: TLO Ltd. This programme is supported by a website with activities and a community to join: http://www.buildinglearningpower.co.uk

Education for Creativity

Creativity, Culture and Education (CCE) is the new national organization created to generate transformational cultural and creative programmes for children and young people across England to enhance their aspirations, achievements, skills and life chances. Their site contains downloadable literature reviews and reports: http://www.creativitycultureeducation.org/

D. Wyse and P. Dowson (2009) *The Really Useful Creativity Book*. London: Routledge offers an excellent introduction to teaching for creativity.

General thinking strategies

Project Zero based at Harvard is a rich source of inspiration and materials: http://pzweb.harvard.edu/

Within this site, Visible Thinking, based on David Perkins' ideas on teaching thinking has many valuable resources: http://pzweb.harvard.edu/vt/VisibleThinking_html_files/01_VisibleThinkingInAction/01a_VTInAction.html

Robert Fisher maintains a useful set of UK resources and links: http://www.teachingthinking.net/

Kestrel Consultants, working with Professor Bob Burden of the University of Exeter, offer training in various thinking strategies in order to become recognized as a thinking school: http://www.thinkingschool.co.uk/

Bibliography

Adey, P. and Shayer, M. (1994) *Really Raising Standards*. London: Routledge.

Adey, P. (ed.) (2008) *Let's Think Handbook: Cognitive Acceleration in the Primary School.* London: nferNelson.

Alexander, R. (2000) *Culture and Pedagogy*. Oxford: Blackwell.

Alexander, R. (2004) *Towards Dialogic Teaching: Rethinking classroom talk*. Cambridge: Dialogos.

Alexander, R. (2006) *Education as Dialogue: Moral and pedagogical choices for a runaway world*. Cambridge: Dialogos.

Alexander, R. (ed.) (2009) *Children, their World, their Education: Final report and recommendations of the Cambridge Review*. London: Routledge.

Anderson, L. and Krathwohl, D. (2001) *A Taxonomy for Learning, Teaching, and Assessing*. New York: Longman.

Archer, M., Bhaskar, R., Collier, A., Lawson, A. and Norrie, A. (eds) (1998) *Critical Realism: Essential readings*. London: Routledge.

Bakhtin, M. (1981) *The Dialogic Imagination*. Austin: University of Texas Press.

Bakhtin, M. (1986) *Speech Genres and Other Late Essays*. Austin: University of Texas Press.

Bhaskar, R. (1997) *A Realist Theory of Science*. London: Verso.

Blakemore, S. J. and Frith, U. (2005) *The Learning Brain: Lessons for education*. Oxford: Blackwell.

Bloom, B. (ed.) (1956) *Taxonomy of Educational Objectives: The classification of educational goals: Handbook I, Cognitive Domain*. New York; Toronto: Longmans, Green.

Bolton, G. and Heathcote, D. (1995) *Drama for Learning: Dorothy Heathcote's Mantle of the Expert Approach to Education* (Dimensions of Drama). London: Heinemann.

Bruns, A. (2008) *Blogs, Wikipedia, Second Life, and Beyond: From production to produsage*. New York: Peter Lang.

Burnard, P., Grainger, T. and Craft, A. (2006) Documenting possibility thinking: A journey of collaborative enquiry. *International Journal of Early Years Education*, Special Issue on *Creativity and Cultural Innovation in Early Childhood Education*, 14(3), 243–262.

Carpenter, P., Just, M. and Shell, P. (1990) What one intelligence test measures: A theoretical account of the processing of the Raven Progressive Matrices test. *Psychological Review*, 9(7), 404–431.

Carter, R. (1999) Common language: Corpus, creativity and cognition. *Language and Literature*, 8(3), 195–216.

Carter, R. (2002) *Language and Creativity*. London: Routledge.

Chi, M. (1997) Creativity: Shifting across ontological categories flexibly. In T. B. Ward, S. M. Smith and J. Vaid (eds) *Creative Thought: An investigation of conceptual structures and processes*. Washington, DC: American Psychological Association.

Chi, M. and Brem, S. (2009) Contrasting Ohlsson's Resubsumption Theory With Chi's Categorical Shift Theory. *Educational Psychologist*, 44(1), 58–63.

Claxton, G. (2002) *Building Learning Power*. Bristol: TLO Ltd.

Claxton, G. (2006) Thinking at the edge: Developing soft creativity. *Cambridge Journal of Education*, 36(3), 351–362.

Claxton, G. (2008) *What is the Point of School?* London: Oneworld Publications.

Claxton, G., Edwards, L. and Scale-Constantinou, V. (2006) Cultivating creative mentalities: A framework for education. *Thinking Skills and Creativity*, 1(1), 57–61.

Craft, A. (2000) *Creativity across the Primary Curriculum: Framing and Developing Practice*. London: RoutledgeFalmer.

Craft, A. (2005) *Creativity in Schools: Tensions and dilemmas*. London: Routledge.

Crandell, L. E. and Hobson, R. P. (1999) Individual Differences in Young Children's IQ: A social-developmental perspective. *Journal of Child Psychology and Psychiatry*, 40, 455–464.

Csíkszentmihályi, M. (1996) *Creativity: Flow and the psychology of discovery and invention*. New York: HarperCollins.

Cunliffe, L. (2008) A Case Study: How Interdisciplinary Teaching Using Information and Communication Technology and Supported by a Creative Partner Impacted on Creativity in an Extra-Curricular School Activity. *International Journal of Education through Art*, 4(1), 91–104.

Dawes, L. (2008) *The Essential Speaking and Listening: Talk for Learning at Key Stage 2*. London: Routledge.

Dawes, L., Mercer, N. and Wegerif, R. (2000) *Thinking Together: A programme of activities for developing speaking, listening and thinking skills for children aged 8–11*. Birmingham: Imaginative Minds Ltd.

De Boo, M. (1999) *Using Science to Develop Thinking Skills at Key Stage 1*. London: National Association for Able Children in Education/David Fulton.

De Laat, M. (2006) *Networked Learning*. Amsterdam: Politie Academy.

Deaney, R., Chapman, A. and Hennessy, S. (2009) A case-study of one teacher's use of an interactive whiteboard system to support knowledge co-construction in the history classroom. *Curriculum Journal*, 20(4), 365–387.

Deridda, J. (1968) La Différance in: *Théorie d'ensemble*. Paris: Éditions de Seuil.

Deridda, J. (1981) *Dissemination* (trans. Barbara Johnson). Chicago: Chicago University Press.

Dunbar, K. (1997) How scientists think: On-line creativity and conceptual change in science. In T. B. Ward, S. M. Smith and J. Vaid (eds) *Creative Thought: An investigation of conceptual structures and processes*. Washington, DC: American Psychological Association.

Edwards, A. (2005) Let's get beyond community and practice: The many meanings of learning by participating. *The Curriculum Journal*, 16(1), 49–65.

Eliot, T. S. (1936) 'Burnt Norton'. Accessed March 2010 from http://www.tristan. icom43.net/quartets/norton.html

Erduran, S., Osborne, J. and Simon, S. (2004) Enhancing the Quality of Argument in School Science. *Journal of Research in Science Teaching*, 41(10), 994–1020.

Faulkner, D., Joubert, M. and Kynan, S. (2006) *Project EXCITE!: Excellence, creativity and innovation in teaching and education Phase II: A longitudinal study of excellence, creativity and innovation in teaching and learning in primary education*. http://www.excite-education.org/

Geirland, J. (1996) Go With The Flow. *Wired Magazine*, September, Issue 4.09.

Gladwell, M. (2008) *Outliers: The story of success*. New York: Little, Brown and Company.

Goody, J. (1977) *The Domestication of the Savage Mind*. Cambridge, England: Cambridge University Press.

Gordon, W. (1961) *Synectics*. New York: Harper and Row.

Grainger, T., Burnard, P. and Craft, A. (2006) Pedagogy and possibility thinking in the Early Years. *Thinking Skills and Creativity*, 1(2), 26–38.

Hand, S. (2009) *Emmanuel Levinas*. London: Routledge.

Heidegger, M. (1969) *Identity and Difference* (bilingual edn, trans. J. Stambaugh). New York: Harper and Row.

Heidegger, M. (1978) *Basic Writings*. London: Routledge.

Higgins, S. (2001) *Thinking Through Primary Teaching*. Cambridge: Chris Kington Publishing.

Hobson, R. P. (2002) *The Cradle of Thought: Exploring the origins of thinking*. London: Macmillan.

Hughes, M. (1990) Children's computation. In R. Grieve and M. Hughes (eds) *Understanding Children*. Oxford: Blackwell.

Ipgrave, J. (2003) Building E-Bridges. Inter-Faith Dialogue by E-mail. *Teaching Thinking*, Summer, Issue 11.

Johnson, S. and Gardner, P. (1999) Some Achilles heels of thinking skills: A response to Higgins and Baumfield. *Journal of Philosophy of Education*, 33(3), 435–449.

Jonassen, D., Carr, C. and Yueh, H. (1998) Computers as Mindtools for Engaging Learners in Critical Thinking, *TechTrends*, 43, 24–32.

Koschmann, T. (ed.) (in press) *Theorizing Practice*. New York: Springer.

Kuhn, D. (2005) *Education for Thinking*. Cambridge, MA: Cambridge University Press.

Kuhn, T. (1962) *The Structure of Scientific Revolutions*. Chicago: University of Chicago Press.

Leat, D. and Higgins, S. (2002) The role of powerful pedagogical strategies in curriculum development. *The Curriculum Journal*, 13(1), 71–85.

Leibniz, G. (1973) *Leibniz: Philosophical Writings* (G. Parkinson (ed.), trans. M. Morris and G. Parkinson). London: Dent and Sons.

Levy, P. (1999) *Collective Intelligence: Mankind's emerging world in cyberspace*. New York: Perseus.

Lipman, M. (2003) *Thinking in Education* (2nd edn). Cambridge: Cambridge University Press.

Loveless, A. (2000) Creativity, visual literacy and information and communications technology. In D. M. Watson and T. Downes (eds) *Communications and Networking in Education: Learning in a networked society*. Norwell, MA: Kluwer Academic.

Loveless, A., Burton, J. and Turvey, K. (2006) Developing conceptual frameworks for creativity, ICT and teacher education. *Thinking Skills and Creativity*, 1(1), 1–11.

McPeck, J. (1981) *Critical Thinking and Education*. New York: St. Martin's Press.

Mead, G. H. (1934) *Mind, Self, and Society: From the Perspective of a Social Behaviorist* (edited, with an Introduction, by Charles W. Morris). Chicago: University of Chicago Press.

Mercer, N. (1995) *The Guided Construction of Knowledge: Talk amongst teachers and learners*. Clevedon: Multilingual Matters.

Mercer, N. and Littleton, K. (2007) *Dialogue and the Development of Children's Thinking: A sociocultural approach*. London: Routledge.

Mercer, N., Dawes, L., Wegerif, R. and Sams, C. (2004) Reasoning as a scientist: Ways of helping children to use language to learn science. *British Educational Research Journal*, 30(3), 367–385.

Mercer, N., Kershner, R., Warwick, P. and Kleine Staarman, J. (2010) Can the Interactive Whiteboard help provide 'dialogic space' for children's collaborative activity? *Language and Education*, 55(1), 350–362.

Merleau-Ponty, M. (1962) *The Phenomenology of Perception* (trans. Colin Smith). London: Routledge.

Merleau-Ponty, M. (1964) *Le Visible et L'Invisible*. Paris: Gallimard.

Merleau-Ponty, M. (1964) *Signs* (trans. Richard McCleary). Evanston, IL: Northwestern University Press.

Merleau-Ponty, M. (1968) *The Visible and the Invisible* (Claude Lefort (ed.), trans. Alphonso Lingis). Evanston, IL: Northwestern University Press.

NACCCE (1999) *All our Futures: Creativity, culture and education: National Advisory Committee on Creative and Cultural Education*. London: DfEE and DCMS.

Naylor, B. and Naylor, S. (2000) *The Snowman's Coat and other Science Questions*. London: Hodder Children's Books.

Papert, P. (1981) *Mindstorms*. Brighton: Harvester.

Peat, A. (2001) Creative Teaching. *Teaching Thinking*, Issue 5 (Autumn), 50–51.

Perkins, D. N. and Salomon, G. (1989) Are cognitive skills context bound? *Educational Researcher*, 18(1), 16–25.

Pinker, S. (1998) *How the Mind Works*. Harmondsworth: Penguin.

Resnick, L. (1987) *Education and Learning to Think*. Washington, DC: National Academy Press.

Resnick, L., Michaels, S. and O'Connor, C. (2010) How (well structured) talk builds the mind. In R. Sternberg and D. Preiss (eds) *Innovations in Educational Psychology: Perspectives on learning, teaching and human development*. New York: Springer.

Ricoeur, P. (1995) *Oneself as Another*. Chicago: University of Chicago Press.

Ritchhart, R. and Perkins, D. (2005) Learning to think: The challenges of teaching thinking. In K. Holyoak and R. G. Morrison (eds) *Cambridge Handbook of Thinking and Reasoning*. Cambridge: Cambridge University Press.

Rose, J. (2009) *Independent Review of the Primary Curriculum*. http://www.dcsf.gov.uk/primarycurriculumreview/

Sawyer, K. (2006) *Explaining Creativity: The science of human innovation*. New York: Oxford University Press.

Sawyer, K. (2007) *Group Genius: The creative power of collaboration*. New York: Basic Books.

Sendak, M. (1963) *Where the Wild Things Are*. Harmondsworth: Puffin Books.

Smith, A. (1998) *Accelerated Learning: Brain-based methods for accelerating motivation and achievement*. London: Network Educational Press.

Sternberg, R. J. (1990) *Metaphors of Mind: Conceptions of the nature of intelligence*. New York: Cambridge University Press.

Tomasello, M., Carpenter, M., Call, J., Behne, T. and Moll, H. (2005) Understanding and Sharing Intentions: The origins of cultural cognition. *Behavior and Brain Science*, 28(5), 675–691.

Topping, K. and Trickey, S. (2007) Collaborative Philosophical Enquiry for School Children: Cognitive Effects at 10–12 Years. *British Journal of Educational Psychology*, 77(2), 271–288.

Toulmin, S. (1958) *The Uses of Argument*. Cambridge, UK: Cambridge University Press.

Trilling, B. and Hood, P. (2001) Learning, Technology and Education Reform in the Knowledge Age, or We're Wired, Webbed and Windowed, Now What?. In C. Paechter, R. Edwards, R. Harrison and P. Twining (eds) *Learning, Space and Identity*. London: Paul Chapman Publishing and The Open University. Also at: http://www.wested.org/cs/we/view/rs/654

Velmans, M. (2000) *Understanding Consciousness*. London: Routledge.

Vygotsky, L. (1986) *Thought and Language* (trans. A. Kozulin). Cambridge, MA: MIT Press.

Webb, N. M., Nemer, K. M. and Ing, M. (2006) Small-group reflections: Parallels between teacher discourse and student behavior in peer-directed groups. *Journal of the Learning Sciences*, 15(1), 63–119.

Wegerif, R. (1996) Using computers to help coach Exploratory Talk across the curriculum. *Computers and Education*, 26(1–3), 51–60.

Wegerif, R. (2003) *Thinking Skills, Technology and Learning: A review of the literature for NESTA FutureLab*. Available at http://www.nestafuturelab.org/papers (accessed 25 July 2009).

Wegerif, R. (2007) *Dialogic, Education and Technology: Expanding the space of learning*. CSCL Series. New Jersey: Springer.

Wegerif, R. and Mercer, N. (1997) Using computer-based text analysis to integrate quantitative and qualitative methods in the investigation of collaborative learning. *Language and Education*, 11(3), 27–35.

Wegerif, R. and Scrimshaw, P. (eds) (1998) *Computers and Talk in the Primary Classroom*. Clevedon, UK: Multilingual Matters.

Wegerif, R. and Mercer, N. (2000) Language for thinking. In H. Cowie, D. Aalsvoort and N. Mercer (eds) *New Perspectives in Collaborative Learning*. Oxford: Elsevier.

Wegerif, R. and Dawes, L. (2004) *Thinking and Learning with ICT: Raising achievement in primary classrooms*. London: Routledge.

Wegerif, R., Mercer, N. and Dawes, L. (1999) From social interaction to individual reasoning: An empirical investigation of a possible sociocultural model of cognitive development. *Learning and Instruction*, 9(5), 493–516.

Wegerif, R., Perez Linares, J., Rojas Drummond, S., Mercer, N. and Velez, M. (2005) Thinking Together in the UK and Mexico: Transfer of an educational innovation. *Journal of Classroom Interaction*, 40(1), 40–47.

Wegerif, R., McLaren, B., Chamrada, M., Scheuer, O., Mansour, N., Mikšátko, J. and Williams, M. (2010) Exploring creative thinking in graphically mediated synchronous dialogues. *Computers and Education*, 54(3), 613–621.

Wells, G. (1986) *The Meaning Makers: Children learning language and using language to learn*. Portsmouth, NH: Heinemann Educational Books.

Wells, G. (1999) *Dialogic inquiry: Towards a sociocultural practice and theory of education*. New York: Cambridge University Press.

Wertsch, J. V. and Kazak, S. (in press) Saying more than you know in instructional settings. In T. Koschmann (ed.) *Theorizing Practice*. New York: Springer.

Williams, S. and Wegerif, R. (2006) *Radical Encouragement: Changing cultures of learning*. Birmingham: Imaginative Minds.

Wittgenstein, L. (1967) *Philosophical Investigations*. Oxford: Blackwell.

Wolfe, S. (2006) Teaching and learning through dialogue in primary classrooms in England. Unpublished PhD thesis, University of Cambridge.

Wyse, D. and Dowson, P. (2009) *The Really Useful Creativity Book*. London: Routledge.

Index

DEVELOPING THINKING; DEVELOPING LEARNING

A Guide to Thinking Skills in Education

Debra McGregor

"This highly informative book provides a comprehensive guide to the teaching of thinking skills in primary and secondary education."
Learning and Teaching Update

It is now recognised that thinking skills, such as problem-solving, analysis, synthesis, creativity and evaluation, can be nurtured and developed, and education professionals can play a significant role in shaping the way that children learn and think. As a result, schools are being encouraged to make greater use of thinking skills in lessons and the general emphasis on cognition has developed considerably. This book offers a comprehensive introduction to thinking skills in education and provides detailed guidance on how teachers can support cognitive development in their classrooms.

Developing Thinking; Developing Learning discusses how thinking programmes, learning activities and teachers' pedagogy in the classroom can fundamentally affect the nature of pupils' thinking, and considers the effects of the learning environment created by peers and teachers. It compares the nature, design and outcomes of established thinking programmes used in schools and also offers practical advice for teachers wishing to develop different kinds of thinking capabilities.

This is an indispensable guide to thinking skills in schools today, and is key reading for education studies students, teachers and trainee teachers, and educational psychologists.

Contents: *List of figures and tables – Acknowledgements – Introduction – What do we mean by 'thinking?' – What kind of thinking should we encourage children to do? – Thinking and learning – The nature of thinking programmes developed within a subject context – The nature of general thinking skills programmes – The nature of infusing thinking – Effectiveness of thinking programmes – Development of creative thinking – Development of critical thinking – Development of metacognition – Development of problem solving capability – Synthesising the general from the particular – Professional development to support thinking classrooms – School development to support thinking communities – References – Index.*

2007   344pp

978-0-335-21780-9 (Paperback) 978-0-335-21781-6 (Hardback)

APPROACHES TO LEARNING

A Guide for Teachers

Anne Jordan, Orison Carlile and Annetta Stack

"This book provides a really sound grounding in the theories that underpin successful teaching and learning. Without over-simplification it provides accessible introductions to the key learning theories with which teachers and students are likely to engage, and it has immense practical value."

> Professor Sally Brown, Pro-Vice-Chancellor,
> Leeds Metropolitan University, UK

This comprehensive guide for education students and practitioners provides an overview of the major theories of learning. It considers their implications for policy and practice and sets out practical guidelines for best pedagogical practice.

The book can be read as a series of stand-alone chapters or as an integrated overview of theoretical perspectives drawn from the philosophy, psychology, sociology and pedagogy that guide educational principles and practice. Each chapter contains:

- An accessible introduction to each theory
- A summary of key principles
- Critical insights drawn from the theories discussed
- Examples and illustrations from contemporary research and practice
- Summary boxes that highlight critical and key points made
- Practical implications for education professionals

Approaches to Learning is an invaluable resource for students and practitioners who wish to reflect on their educational constructs and explore and engage in the modern discourse of education.

Contents: *List of figures and tables – Acknowledgements – Introduction – Philosophy of education – Behaviourism – Cognitivism – Constructivism – Social learning – Cultural learning – Intelligence – Life course development – Adult learning – Values – Motivation – The learning body – Language and learning – Experiential and competency-based learning – Inclusivity – Blended learning – The future – Glossary.*

2008   304pp

978-0-335-22670-2 (Paperback) 978-0-335-22671-9 (Hardback)